The
Stock Market
Mercenary
BEATING THE INSIDERS
AT THEIR OWN GAME

By
Daniel L. James, M.B.A.

Writers Closet
a division of TrakSoft
PO Box 6652
Lakeland, Florida 33807-6652
863-709-8792
Fax: 407-386-7747

Published by **Writers Closet**
a division of TrakSoft
Post Office Box 6652
Lakeland, Florida 33807-6652
www.WritersCloset.com

The Stock Market Mercenary
BEATING THE INSIDERS AT THEIR OWN GAME

ISBN 0-9742416-8-7

Printed in the United States of America.

2003: e-Book version (ISBN 0-9742416-1-X)
2006: 1st Printing

1 2 3 4 5 6 7 8 9 0

About the Author

Daniel L. James is an Information Technology Executive with over twenty-six years of professional consulting and systems analysis experience. He has a Master of Business Administration degree, specializing in Information Technology Management, and is CEO and Senior Consultant for Larkin Industries, Inc., a privately held Nevada-based firm offering management consulting, software development, research, and on-site training services.

His clients have included Dow Jones Top 30 Industrials, Fortune 500 firms, corporate startups, and numerous private companies and individuals.

In the 1970s, Mr. James began to research investment methods, initially in the commodities futures markets, and was able to capitalize on the Gold Rally of the late 70's, by buying Krugerrand futures at $270 per ounce in early-1979 and selling at $650 per ounce in January, 1980, leveraging a 15% margin into 938% returns. His subsequent research of equity markets uncovered clear patterns and signals assisting him in making market predictions for his own investments. In 1987, as co-publisher of *California Grower* magazine, Mr. James began to write about some troubling trends in the economy. In September, he submitted a "Perspective" column to *California Grower* for publication in the November 1987 issue (Vol. XI, No. 11) in which he warned his readers to prepare for a crisis, based on indicators that paralleled the Crash of 1929. An excerpt from that warning follows:

> ...[U]nder the present system of leveraged credit, it doesn't take many bank insolvencies to generate a nationwide lending crisis. Should such a crisis emerge, the last thing farmers need is to be mortgaged to the hilt.
>
> Some troubling parallels have emerged by comparing current events with the causes and effects of the banking crisis of 1929. Although many conclusions can be drawn from the facts, an important question persists. Could there be another major breakdown in the banking system?
>
> ...The Crash of 1929 occurred at the apex of an eight-year bull market in which stock dividend yields were 3 percent or lower. Latin America loan defaults were a daily news item. Mutual funds (known then as 'investment trusts') multiplied like rabbits. Investment-related debt levels broke every historical record. Oil prices fell 25 percent in the three years before the crash. A huge trade deficit and mounting protectionism were the political topics. Sound familiar?
>
> Our present bull market is in its sixth year. Stocks are currently yielding about three percent. On February 21, 1987, Brazil suspended all interest payments on its $108 billion debt - owed mostly to U.S. banks. ...Add to this Argentina's $53 billion, Venezuela's $32 billion, and Mexico's $96 billion, all in default. In total, including all third-world and Soviet bloc countries, over $1.2 trillion is owed. Mutual funds are the rage nowadays - a new fund joins the market almost every day. The total consumer and investment-related debt in the U.S. has tripled in the last decade. Oil prices have fallen about 30 percent over the past three years. And trade deficits and protectionism are once again hot political issues.

...Will you be able to survive a crisis even if [your bankers and suppliers] cannot? Yes, if you stay informed, understand the big picture, know the warning signs, and plan accordingly.[1]

The magazine hit the stands in late-October, unfortunately, a few days too late to help the readers. On "Black Monday," October 19, 1987, the Dow Jones[SM] lost 508 points, representing more than a 22-percent single-day decline. From the Dow's posted high of 2,747 on August 25th, the Black Monday drop meant an overall loss of nearly 1,070 points, or 38 percent. The next day (October 20th), the Dow sank another 61 points, resulting in a two-day crash of over 25 percent, and a 56-day loss of about 41 percent.[2]

Since that time, Mr. James has continued to research and publish his findings and opinions about the economy and the markets through newsletters, and to consult privately with individual investors. He also advises various corporate and individual investment portfolio managers who are employing the techniques described in this book.

Mr. James is neither a licensed stock analyst nor a broker. As he documents in this book, becoming an SEC-licensed market professional means one must espouse a particular "dogma" to the exclusion of other proven investment strategies.

To learn more about Dan James, please visit his website at www.DLJames.com or at www.StockMarketMercenary.com.

---

[1] Dan James. "Credit: The American Way; Depression: Are We On The Way?" California Grower, November 1987, Vol. XI, No. 11, pp. 37-38.

[2] Source: Dow Jones Industrial Average, Wall Street Journal, 2003. Looking back from the 2003 Dow, the split-adjusted point drop on Black Monday would have been 486.6 points (from 2,164.2 to 1,677.6).

To Cynthia,
my longsuffering soul mate,
with love.

Table of Contents

Acknowledgements

First, I would like to thank my M.B.A. advisor, Lee E. Hargrave, Jr., for his encouragement and guidance in the development of my original paper, titled *Contrarian Investing: Riding the Manipulators' Coattails* (www.DLJames.com). This book is a much-expanded and updated version of that paper. Mr. Hargrave is the author of *Plan For Profitability! How To Write a Strategic Business Plan* (Four Seasons Publishers, 1999), which was one of my textbooks at Rushmore University. Oh yes: thanks for the "A" Professor!

One of the textbooks I used in researching my M.B.A. paper on investing was *101 Investment Lessons from the Wizards of Wall Street* (The Career Press, 1999), by Michael Sincere. I appreciate Mike's encouragement to further develop and publish my methods, and for the opportunity to preview the manuscript of his latest book for beginning stock traders, *Understanding Stocks* (McGraw-Hill, 2003). I highly recommend it.

A special thanks goes to my consulting colleague and publisher, Gary A. Harris (Writers Closet, a division of TrakSoft, Lakeland, Florida), for lighting a fire under my tail to get this book finished.

I appreciate all the help and encouragement from my fellow "mercenaries" who have followed my trades for the past few years and who have witnessed real profits, even during market declines. A giant thanks is due my statistical analysis team at *Larkin* for the countless hours of program development to simulate human trading patterns, resulting in extremely accurate tests of popular trading strategies.

I am deeply grateful to *Yahoo! Inc* and to *Larkin Industries, Inc.*, (LarkinSoft) for permission to use their stock charts and other content embedded throughout this book. Some online chart sources were unwilling to risk their reputations on a book this controversial; *Yahoo!* and *Larkin* were the exceptions.

Finally, thanks to the authors of the many references used in this book - I hope I have adequately credited you for the quotes and concepts gleaned from your excellent works.

---Dan James, Spring, 2003

Legalese (a "must read")

The investment methods and techniques described in this book were developed for, and are based on, the author's financial circumstances, goals and tolerance to risk. In the securities or commodities markets, there are, of course, no guarantees of profitability regardless of the methods used.

Investment in stocks or commodity futures for potential profit is accompanied by the risk of loss of the entire investment. One cannot consistently predict future results from past performance, although many try. Therefore, the investments you make should be based on your particular financial circumstances, goals and tolerance to risk.

Throughout this book, masculine pronouns may appear without a corresponding feminine pronoun. The intent is to include all genders in these references while saving you from having to read awkward "his/her" and "he or she" phrases. Please do not be offended if I omit your favorite pronoun!

Nothing in this book is intended to accuse specific corporate insiders or investment professionals of intentionally unethical or illegal practices. In most cases, the manipulations discussed herein are simply consequences of the existing capitalist system. However, if you **are** a corporate insider or investment professional that feels threatened or accused by the evidence presented in this work, or you just generally have a guilty conscience, be aware that this book is designed to help your victims beat you. Sleep well!

Chapter 1: Introduction & Mission

Why do we need yet another stock investment book?

Since the birth of Capitalism in the 17th Century, a war has been waged against the most vulnerable and least-prepared class of investor - the common, individual, public shareholder. The weapons and tactics used in this war have evolved over time, but the effect is the same: *the insiders make huge profits at the expense of the masses.* Today, stock brokers, financial analysts, investment "gurus," television commentators, institutional fund managers, corporate insiders, and - yes - even the federal government are in on the war. Some participants are aware of their roles as accomplices, while others assist unwittingly. Laws to protect individual shareholders are passed and refined every year, but the results are the same. **During any given year, less than seven percent of all stock traders in the United States actually make a profit from their investments.**[3]

I should know. I was one of the 93-percent without a clue. When I started to build a retirement portfolio many years ago, I was unprepared for an entire industry of licensed experts, backed by a federally-protected dogma, and a systematic wealth-erosion machine, dedicated to helping me lose all of my capital.

Don't get me wrong - I love capitalism with its inherent moral and practical freedom. The basic premise of capitalism, as applied to public companies, is clear and simple. Corporations exist for the purpose of making a profit. Without profit, they cannot grow or improve. Any corporation that does not have "making a profit" as its primary motive, will, more sooner than later, go under. On the other hand, stock investors buy stocks for the purpose of making a profit. Without profit, they cannot increase their retirement accounts, pay for the kids' college, or pay for the luxuries of life. Any stock investor that does not have "making a profit" as his primary motive, will, more sooner than later, lose all his capital. This is the real world. This is capitalism.

In most cases, the motives to profit by both corporations and stock investors are compatible. When a corporation profits, the perceived value of its stock rises, the stock price goes up, and the stockholder's investment grows. Conversely, if a corporation loses money, the perceived value of its stock drops, the stock price goes down, and the stockholder's investment shrinks.

That's the *plan*, at least. It sounds clean and simple, and in a perfect world such a system would be "efficient." An unfettered free market tends to naturally weed out those who abuse others, even those who *legally* abuse. Unfortunately, it is not a perfect world, not everyone plays by the plan, some companies misrepresent their profits, there are those who abuse the system, and - as a result - the stock market is definitely **not** efficient. And market regulators often fail to anticipate the long-term effects of their "reforms," granting license (or loopholes) instead to those who would (and do) profit unfairly from information not transparent to the public.

---

[3] Source: Internal Revenue Service (www.irs.gov)

Anyone can be a victim. A person's education and IQ are irrelevant. In my case, the libraries and college finance courses weren't much help. Instead of preparing me for the realities of the markets, I learned only abstract theories. The investment books I read, courses I attended, popular strategies I uncovered, and trading advice I received from professionals, delivered flawed or, at best, incomplete methods. No matter what I thought I knew, I lost money in the stock market, except for a few lucky hits. In the mid-1980s, I realized that my training in stock trading was actually leading me to do the *opposite* of what profitable investing dictated. Instead of using logic - the core skill in the computer profession - I was being led to make my investment decisions emotionally. Apparently, I wasn't alone. I rarely had the occasion to meet a consistently successful stock trader. While I had profited from other investments, including commodities trading, I was "capital gains challenged" with equities.

My resulting frustration motivated a fact-finding quest, spanning nearly 18 years of research into equities trading methods, market statistics, and corporate histories, finally culminating in the information you will learn in this book. Of course, simply writing a book does not automatically make one an "expert" and I make no such claim. I have simply done the homework that - in my opinion - all stock traders should do before risking a dime of capital: **find out who is succeeding in the market, learn everything you can about them, discover their methods, and ride their coattails.** What I discovered in this quest, I now share with you. It is for your financial survival and mine that this effort is dedicated.

The Emotions of Finance

Pick up any book on stock investing and you will see a warning about human emotions. Since I am loathe to break this trend, let me say that, in the financial world, there are three basic human emotions: *Greed*, *Fear*, and *Greed*. OK, so there are a few other human emotions at our disposal, but none have a more potent influence on members of a capitalistic society than greed and fear. This is especially true in matters pertaining to the stock market. Greed causes us to buy "hot" stocks and hold them beyond realistic levels, while fear of loss causes us to sell at the worst possible time. But emotions aren't the only obstacle.

From the start, investors have gambled on the future outcomes of companies while insiders have attempted to "corner the market" and siphon huge fortunes from the wealth of others. Over the years, regulations and organized stock exchanges have restricted the methods used to manipulate the markets, and the mass media has made corporate activities more transparent. But corporations have attempted to cleverly mask their activities from the public, especially those activities that - if widely known - would reverse the fortunes of the corporate insiders. Recent cases such as Enron, Global Crossing and K-Mart are prime examples of this sort of deceptive stockholder manipulation.

In my own case, I realized that I was one of those being routinely manipulated. I needed a crash course in "survival training." The more I studied, the more I found that the manipulation tactics were fully institutionalized at every level, from the stock exchange floor to the brokerages to the media to the government. To win, I had to use the same tactics. But first, I had to *unlearn* the orthodox strategies taught in finance courses and advocated by investment experts. Then, I had to take control of my emotions, especially the one called *greed*.

Despite every effort to regulate the stock market, and to protect investors from themselves, the core activity of the world's largest *casino* has continued unabated - gambling - but under the alias of "speculating." Based on my personal observation, speculators are really investors without discipline. They are easily swayed by media headlines and are constant prey to market predators. From speculators we receive advice such as "buy the rumor, sell the news," and variations thereof. They tend to be the least informed, yet the most aggressive, of traders I've encountered. Throughout history, speculators have lent credence to the *Greater Fool Theory*, which holds that, no matter what price I pay for a stock, there is a greater fool than me willing to pay an even higher price.

Assuming we have decided to stop gambling in the markets, obtain the proper training, and overcome the obstacles of greed, fear and market manipulation, we will then encounter two more enemies attacking our capital: *taxes* and *inflation*. It's no wonder that so many Americans would rather keep their money under the mattress than invest in the stock market.[4] This raises the fundamental question: *Why should we invest in America's companies?*

Who better to answer than the person recognized as one of the modern world's greatest investors, and presently the second-richest man on the planet,[5] Warren Buffett, who summed up his view of wealth-building as follows:

> If a graduating MBA were to ask me, `How do I get rich in a hurry?' I would not respond with quotations from Ben Franklin or Horatio Alger, but would instead hold my nose with one hand and point with the other toward Wall Street.[6]

In other words, the stock market is a potentially dangerous place to make a lot of money very quickly. The problem is, **the very emotions that define our humanity are often used against us by those who attempt to influence our investment decisions**. For every story of someone making it big in the stock market, it seems, there are untold thousands who lose money there. Could it be that all these market losers are stupid? Or, do they simply not do their homework before investing? Are they uneducated? Or, are they educated with the wrong advice? On the matter of education and the "market efficiency" theories taught in schools, Warren Buffett expressed his gratitude:

> It has been helpful to me to have tens of thousands (of students) turned out of business schools taught that it didn't do any good to think.[7]

The Sad Truth about Stock Traders

In May of 1997, the Congressional Budget Office (CBO) published a study in which the capital gains of U.S. taxpayers were analyzed to determine the ratios of gains versus losses.[8] After adjusting for inflation and removing any *loss limits* imposed by the tax system, the CBO concluded that 94.3 percent of those filing capital gains forms routinely lost money. Specifically focusing on corporate stocks and mutual funds, the same study calculated that 93.4 percent of

---

[4] Ibid. In 1997, only ten percent of U.S. taxpayers invested in the stock market. That percentage has grown considerably since then, but still remains under one-third of all taxpayers.

[5] Source: Forbes.com, 2002; "The World's Billionaires" (www.forbes.com/2002/02/28/billionaires.html)

[6] Warren Buffett, quoted by David A. Vise and Steve Coll, "Buffett-watchers Follow Lead of Omaha's Long-term Stock Investor," *The Washington Post*, October 2, 1987, p. D1

[7] Warren Buffett, quoted by Linda Grant, "The $4 Billion Regular Guy," The Los Angeles Times Magazine, April 7, 1991, p. 36.

[8] Congressional Budget Office, May 1997, "Perspectives on the Ownership of Capital Assets and the Realization of Capital Gains." (www.cbo.gov)

U.S. filers suffered losses in *real* dollars.[9] During the decade before, and the five years since the CBO study, investment results have not shown any significant deviation. In fact, millions of new investors, lured to the market by the dot-com craze, lost Trillions. But, not everyone in America is a shareholder.

What about people who save and invest over a lifetime? Are Americans retiring ahead of the game? Sadly, the answer is no. According to the Social Security Administration (SSA), the evidence is clear that there are more financial "losers" than "winners" among retirement-age citizens in this country. In 2000, the SSA found that nearly 30 percent of U.S. citizens, 55 and older, earned below the poverty line. The same study found that over 43 percent of the same age group were living below the poverty line, or within 25 percent of the poverty line. Finally, *over half* of all citizens, 65 and older, were forced to continue working to make ends meet.[10]

These studies indicate that, either the public is getting the wrong advice or they are not following the right advice.

An Old Fashioned Secret

Almost everyone has heard the cliché, "buy low, sell high," and, for over two centuries, this advice has proven itself, if only to a small minority of investors. While the practice has been around since the beginning of capitalism, apparently a form of that phrase originated with Hetty Green, the richest woman in the world in the late 1800s, and one of the forty richest Americans ever. Hetty had turned a modest inheritance into incredible wealth. Considered a genius at making money, she was often asked for words of wisdom, and on one such occasion she offered:

> Before deciding on an investment I seek out every kind of information about it. There is no great secret in fortune making. All you have to do is buy cheap and sell dear, act with thrift and shrewdness and be persistent.[11]

Even back in Hetty's day, successful investors knew the correct method. Today, most traders only give lip service to the phrase, "buy low, sell high." They may believe the advice is true, but they don't follow it. It's not "sexy;" it's not "hot." Somehow, old advice is considered outdated, old fashioned, even though *truth* can never become "outdated," as unpopular as it may be. But, after years of research and statistical analysis of the markets, and personal experience with real money, I have proven (to myself, at least) that average people like us can consistently make a profit in the stock market.

How? By first realizing that those 93-percent of stock traders lose money for a very important reason: **they follow the wrong advice**. Here's the logic: *Since most stock traders act on the advice of brokers, market analysts, financial publications and TV market commentators, and since most stock traders lose money, it must follow that such advice is incorrect most of the time.*

---

[9] Ibid. "Loss limits" require that you artificially limit the amount of capital losses you can deduct, but require all of your gains to be reported. In the CBO study, gains of $13.3 billion were reported with loss limits, representing losses of $28.4 billion without loss limits. Taxpayers are forced to carry forward some of their losses to future tax years in order to offset future gains. "Real" dollars in the CBO report were adjusted for inflation, without loss limit restrictions.

[10] Social Security Administration, "Income of the Population 55 or Older, 2000" (www.ssa.gov)

[11] Hetty Green, quoted by John Steele Gordon, 1999. "The Great Game" (Scribner, New York, NY), pp.154-155.

Am I over-simplifying? Perhaps. Some might argue that, the reason most stock traders lose money is because they *fail to follow* the advice of those market professionals. However, this argument is weak, because some very successful trading strategies are routinely discredited or discarded in favor of a particular "orthodoxy," resulting in a "monopoly of ideas." (More on that "orthodoxy" later.) Thus, the majority of stock traders receive *only* a certain kind of advice. Not being privy to every possible trading strategy, they are asked to make a red-or-black bet on an all-red roulette wheel. Regardless of the side of this argument you choose, these are the facts - there is a *uniformity* of advice offered to the public, and most public stock traders lose money. These results alone make the case for a *Contrarian* approach to investing.

What's a Stock Market Mercenary?

When I say *Contrarian*, however, I do not mean always taking actions that are "contrary" to the market; just "contrary" to the advice of those who have misinformed us. In essence, I am advocating a "mercenary" approach. Now, there are two definitions of that word.[12] One is a noun describing *a hired soldier serving a country other than his own*. The other - the one I have adopted - is an adjective meaning *inspired merely by a desire for gain*. So, the market is going to do what the market is going to do, and a *Stock Market Mercenary* will do what is necessary to profit from the market, even if the methods are "contrary" to orthodox wisdom and advice.

It is often a lonely job, being a *Contrarian*. I've lost count of the phone calls from stockbrokers through the years, "encouraging" me to buy a particular stock that's "hot" or on which the broker has "uncovered inside information." Instead of just saying "no thanks" and hanging up, I sometimes messed with their minds before disappointing them. First, I asked them if the stock was currently on an uptrend, a downtrend, a sideways pattern at the top, or a sideways pattern at the bottom. (In most cases, a "hot" stock is either on a steep uptrend or has already reached the top and is going sideways.) Next, I asked how many shares of this stock the broker currently owned, or had ever owned. If the broker said "None," I asked, "Why not?" If the broker owned it in the past, but had recently sold it, I asked, "Why are you trying to get me to buy it then?" The third option (that the broker owned the stock and hadn't sold it), has yet to happen! In any case, by now, the broker had usually answered his own question as to why I wasn't interested in his "hot" stock. I'm afraid that stockbrokers do not particularly like *Stock Market Mercenaries*, especially those with a sense of humor!

This book is designed to show you the mindset of a *mercenary*, which - if adopted - will help you make a profit from your stock market investments. But you must start your training from the beginning.

Your Mission

The purpose of this book is to:

1. Illustrate the effects of government imposed "wealth erosion" forces on our capital, rendering traditional investment returns totally insufficient;

2. Offer overwhelming evidence supporting the premise that the investing public is routinely manipulated, causing them to make poor trading decisions;

---

[12] The New Lexicon Webster's Dictionary of the English Language, 1988 Edition (Lexicon Publications, Inc., New York, NY)

3. Compare the most popular stock trading strategies and expose their fatal flaws that help the unwary lose their capital;

4. Offer evidence that the government imposes a dogma - a gag order, of sorts - that often prevents the public from receiving profitable advice; and

5. Suggest strategies and tactics to overcome these obstacles, allowing us "outsiders" to survive and prosper in the stock market.

Your mission is to read each chapter in the order presented. Don't even *think* about skipping to the end to find out some trading methods before first learning to defend yourself against the enemies of wealth that surround you. Tactics and weapons must go together, and *knowledge* is the weapon of choice for a *Stock Market Mercenary*.

Unfortunately, many people who read this book - even if they totally agree with its conclusions - will not change their investment habits. It takes a lot of intestinal fortitude to buck the flood of advice from friends, relatives, superiors, stockbrokers, and the pundits and touts on the morning market shows. Not everyone has the constitution to be a *Stock Market Mercenary*. I didn't either, at first. But I was determined to become part of the seven percent of investors that actually make a profit year after year, and I found the weapons to make it happen.

"One thing in favor of death over taxes -- death doesn't get worse every time Congress meets."

--Judge Jacob M. Braude

Chapter 2: The Enemies of Wealth

How the Government taxes both our capital and our gains.

It has been said that there are only two guarantees in life: death and taxes. It is not difficult to understand death - we have all felt its effects in our families at one time or another. I am constantly amazed, though, at how little taxpayers understand the effects of taxation on their wealth, especially the "hidden tax" known as *inflation*. The problem with taxes is that, to a capitalist, they are always too high; they reduce the profitability of success and, thus, stunt the future growth of business or investment capital. The problem with inflation is that it's hard to determine in advance what the "tax rate" is going to be - all you know is that your existing capital will not buy as much next year as it could this year, meaning an effective reduction of wealth; meaning a tax. We know that inflation exists, but we don't easily see it for what it is. Thus, *inflation is a tax that's been hidden in plain sight.*

I cannot overstress the importance, if you wish to succeed financially, of knowing the reasons why, and how, your wealth is being targeted. As the great Chinese general, Sun Tzu, stated in *The Art of War*, originally written more than 2,500 years ago:

> If you know the enemy and know yourself, you need not fear the result of a hundred battles. If you know yourself but not the enemy, for every victory gained you will also suffer a defeat. If you know neither the enemy nor yourself, you will succumb in every battle.[13]

The Stock Market Mercenary must know with certainty the weapons used against his capital, so that investment plans and strategies can be devised to overcome them. And the first weapon in the opposition's arsenal is the *Inflation Machine*. Brace yourself - portions of this chapter might make you angry. But that could be a *good* thing!

The Inflation Machine

The *results* of inflation are all around us; for example:

- Loss of purchasing power (a dollar doesn't buy what it used to);

- Higher and higher cost of living;

- Tax bracket creep (as your salary increases to keep up, you move to higher tax brackets); and

- Loss of asset value (the longer you hold your assets, the less they are worth in inflation-adjusted dollars).

---

[13] Clavell, James, editor. 1983. "The Art of War: Sun Tzu" Dell Publishing, New York, NY; edited from translation by Lionel Giles, 1910, Shanghai.

Although we notice these results, most people do not directly associate them with inflation. Perhaps if they knew the *cause* of inflation, they could make the connection. I, therefore, offer the following definition: *In any economy, inflation is the rate at which the nation's total money supply grows within a given period.*

Right about now, the economists among you will stop me and show me formulas that correlate the "rate of inflation" with the Gross Domestic Product (GDP), the Consumer Price Index (CPI), or other widely accepted metrics. Unfortunately, these indexes measure the changes in the overall market value of assets, goods and services, but do not accurately measure the actual reduction in purchasing power - which is the hidden-tax effect of inflation. Only an increase in money supply can cause true inflation. But don't take **my** word for it.

In 1999, the Federal Reserve Bank of Cleveland published a document titled *Money Growth and Inflation*, which studied the "Quantity Theory" - the belief that money supply changes and inflation changes have a one-to-one relationship. The sources used in this study included Federal Reserve Banks, the Congressional Budget Office, the U.S. Treasury, and other agencies. The report included many charts showing this correlation, but one in particular - a 40-year chart - best illustrated the point (see Figure 2-1). The Fed's report concluded the issue as follows:

> The quantity theory of money provides a clear prediction about the relationship between money growth and inflation, asserting that money supply growth is the primary factor determining the inflation rate. In its strictest form, the theory holds that inflation increases one-for-one with money growth. Over long-term horizons, the quantity theory has been an empirical success. The average rates of money growth and inflation over long periods of time and across many countries show a striking one-to-one connection between money growth and inflation, as predicted by the quantity theory.[14]

In a 1997 study, published by the Congressional Budget Office (CBO), the combined effects of inflation and capital gains tax laws were clearly described, using the 1993 tax year as an example. Note the distinction made between the "real" value of assets and the "nominal" (apparent) value of assets.

> In time, inflation tends to increase the nominal value of assets, leading to an overstatement of the real gain. Correcting for inflation over the period in which assets are held reduces the value of realized capital gains and even converts many nominal capital gains into real capital losses. Calculations based on a simple inflation adjustment show that, on average, the sale of capital gains assets realized ... was substantially lower than the inflation-adjusted purchase price. That calculation, however, does not reflect the current-law loss limit. Taking account of that loss limit, capital assets other than bonds generated net capital gains of $81.4 billion, on average, before adjustment for inflation but only $39.5 billion once that adjustment was made. Thus, since inflation-adjusted capital gains amounted to about one-half of nominal gains in 1993, the effective tax rate on inflation-adjusted gains was about twice the rate currently applied to nominal gains.[15]

---

[14] Federal Reserve Bank, Cleveland, July 1999, "Money Growth and Inflation" (PUB Cleveland, July 1999)
[15] Congressional Budget Office, May 1997, "Perspectives on the Ownership of Capital Assets and the Realization of Capital Gains." (www.cbo.gov)

Did you catch that? The CBO found that the effective tax rate on inflation-adjusted gains was about **twice** the rate normally applied to gains. This means that, over a long period, inflation doubles the taxes we pay!

Inflation, percent

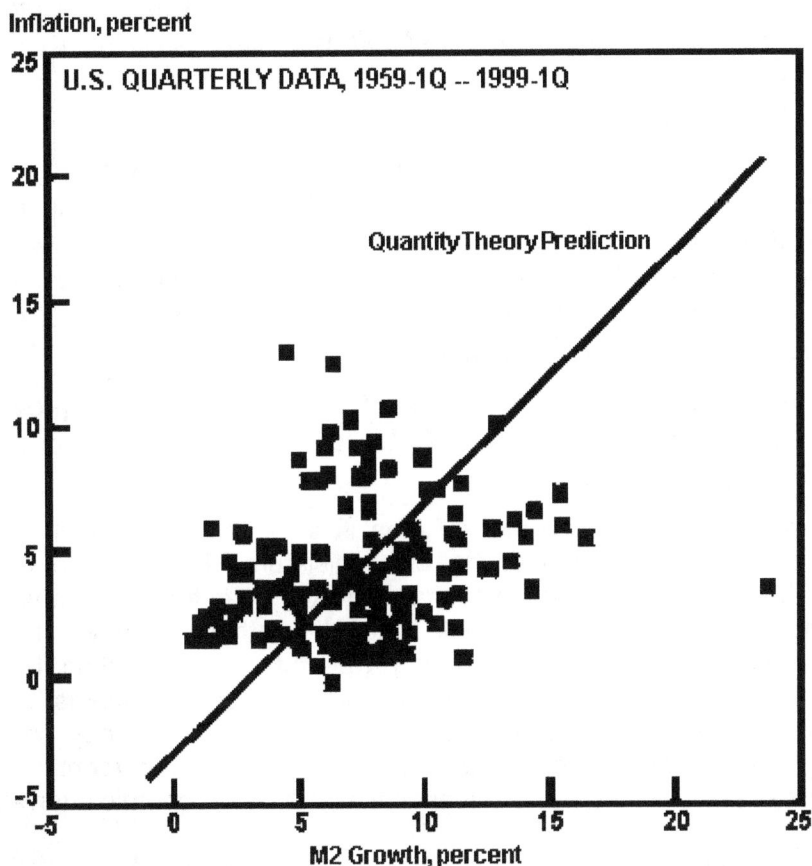

FIGURE 2-1. **Correlation of money growth and inflation. Data marks represent the relationship between money growth and the inflation rate for each of the 40 years surveyed. "M2" is defined as the sum of currency, travelers checks, demand deposits, and other checkable deposits, plus retail, money market, mutual fund, savings, and small time deposits. Source: Federal Reserve Bank, Cleveland.**

According to the Federal Reserve, "M3," the total American money supply (currency and institutional account balances worldwide containing U.S. dollars) has grown from $292 billion in 1959 to a little over $8.5 Trillion as of the end of 2002.[16] This represents an average annual growth rate (AAG) of just over **eight percent**! Although the "official" indexed inflation rate has been touted at or below three percent since 1995, the *true* inflation rate - increase in money supply - has been over nine percent since 1995.[17] In the 1970s, the *true* inflation rate soared to 14.21 percent, while in 1992 the rate dropped to a deflationary minus 0.23 percent.

---

[16] Federal Reserve, "Money Stock and Debt Measures" (March 22, 2001). Based on "M3" money supply, including all currency, deposit instruments, and institutional "U.S. dollar" balances worldwide. A supplement to this report, "H.6 Release -- Federal Reserve Board of Governors" (http://research.stlouisfed.org/fred/data/wkly/m3) is updated weekly on the Internet.

[17] Most official "inflation" estimates are based on the growth of "M1" which includes only currency, travelers checks, demand deposits, and other checkable deposits. This number ignores the "computer money" deposited in banks, insurance companies, credit unions, mutual funds, money markets, and foreign banks (i.e., Eurodollars).

What does inflation have to do with purchasing power? Simple: when the money supply is *diluted* over time, prices of goods and services and costs-of-living rise proportionally. For example, based on an eight-percent growth rate in the money supply, *a one-dollar bill in 1959 is today worth about three cents*. Put another way, *what cost a buck in 1959 would cost over $30 today. If a decent year's salary in 1959 were $8,000, you would need to earn around $220,000 today to buy the same quality of life.* How many of us can claim that rate of growth in our salaries over the same period?

For the sake of comparison, consider gold, which maintains its value by being "inflation-proof." For example, one hundred years ago you could buy a rifle and some ammunition for an ounce of gold. Today, you can buy a rifle and some ammunition for an ounce of gold. It isn't *gold* that has changed in value in a hundred years, but our purchasing power that's been diluted through inflation. Now you know why many *hedge fund* managers use gold to preserve value during volatile markets or periods of geopolitical turmoil.

In an article written for Fortune Magazine in 1977, Warren Buffett expressed his concerns about inflation in a manner that *even I* could understand. Read his statement a couple of times and do the math in your head. It's amazing:

> The arithmetic makes it plain that inflation is a far more devastating tax than anything that has been enacted by our legislature. The inflation tax has a fantastic ability to simply consume capital. It makes no difference to a widow with her savings in a 5 percent passbook account whether she pays 100 percent income tax on her interest income during a period of zero inflation, or pays no income taxes during years of 5 percent inflation. Either way, she is 'taxed' in a manner that leaves her no real income whatsoever. Any money she spends comes right out of capital. She would find outrageous a 120 percent income tax, but doesn't seem to notice that 5 percent inflation is the economic equivalent.[18]

Therefore, to "break even" from inflation, we must either receive a cost-of-living increase in our wages equal to the percentage increase in the money supply, or we must earn *excess* profits from investments to counter the erosion from inflation. But what is the benefit of merely breaking even? None. *To build up wealth in preparation for retirement, we must get ahead of both taxes and inflation.* So far, we have dealt with inflation at its most "arcane" level. Next, let's examine what taxes and inflation really do to our personal finances.

The Mathematics of Capital Erosion

I like to challenge my friends and colleagues (too often, I'm told) to estimate their current total tax rate. Most reply with, "I'm in the 16 percent tax bracket" or "I paid 33 percent in federal income tax last year." So, I have them add up all the other taxes they pay, such as Social Security, Unemployment, Disability, Medicare,[19] State Income Tax, Capital Gains Tax on investment returns and dividends, Property Tax, Sales Tax, and Excise Taxes on phone and utility bills. By now, their eyes are wide open as they see how much of their paycheck is taken each year. If they have large deductions, I point out the perils of the Alternative Minimum Tax, required of those who have legitimate deductions but whose gross income is somehow deemed

---

[18] Warren E. Buffett, May 5, 1977. "How Inflation Swindles the Investor" (Fortune), p. 250.
[19] Yes, I know, some of the deductions listed are really "insurance-type deductions," but, if it walks like a duck and talks like a duck...

"too high."[20] Then, I hit them with *inflation tax* on all pre-existing capital, plus a pro-rated amount on accumulated gains throughout the year.

Before your eyes glaze over here, let me simplify these calculations with an actual exercise I did with a fellow consultant, a resident of the Golden State of California -- we'll call him Jack. My friend earned approximately $100,000 in adjusted gross annual salary, plus he was earning 10 percent annual returns on about $100,000 in a non-tax-deferred mutual fund (no comment!). Finally, Jack had $15,000 in a savings account earning 3.5 percent (still no comment!). Jack was proud of these returns, mind you, and figured he was doing better than the average Californian. He was probably right. Looking at the 2001 tax tables, for a married couple, filing jointly, we calculated that Jack was in the 21.67 percent federal tax bracket, after major deductions. Our resulting calculations are depicted in Figure 2-2.

Adjusted Gross Income:	100,000		**Mutual Fund Capital:**	100,000
Federal Income Tax:	(21,670)		Est. Inflation on Prior Capital:	(8,000)
FICA (Social Security):	(4,985)		Profit on Investment:	10,000
State Income Tax:	(6,300)		Capital Gains Tax:	(2,800)
All other Fed/State Deductions:	(1,500)		Est. Inflation on Profit:	(433)
Pre-Inflation Net Salary:	65,545		**"REAL" Net Profit:**	(1,233)
Est. Inflation Cost of Net Salary:	(2,840)			
Net Profit from All Investments:	(2,078)		**Cash in Savings:**	15,000
"REAL" Net Income:	60,627		Est. Inflation on Prior Capital:	(1,200)
			Interest Earned:	525
			Tax on Interest Earned:	(147)
			Est. Inflation on Interest Earned:	(23)
			"REAL" Net Profit:	(845)
SUMMARY				
TOTAL GROSS INCOME:	110,525			
LESS TOTAL TAXES:	(37,402)	**(34%) Tax Bracket**		
LESS TOTAL INFLATION:	(12,496)	**(11%) Inflation Bracket**		
"REAL" NET INCOME:	60,627			

FIGURE 2-2. Jack's example, illustrating the effects of taxes and inflation on his income and capital. Note that the amount deducted for Social Security (the "Payroll Tax") is only Jack's portion - his employer voluntarily paid an additional $4,985.

This exercise revealed that *Jack was really in a 45 percent tax and inflation bracket!* Further, he was actually losing money, after inflation, on both his mutual fund and savings account investments. The bottom line for Jack was that he worked for the Government through June 13th of each year, and worked the rest of the year for himself. By the end of the year, out of $110,525 in total revenues, Jack had the purchasing power of just $60,627. His "tax bracket" was actually 34 percent, not 21.67 percent. And, when the total *dollar amount* lost to inflation from all his

---

[20] The AMT was initiated in the 1960's to catch 155 high-income taxpayers who had figured out the tax system. Today, over 2,000,000 taxpayers are caught in the AMT trap, thanks to tax bracket creep, and that number is rising rapidly.

capital, profits and salary was subtracted from his gross income, the effect this *tax* had on his purchasing power was devastating.

An interesting revelation was that, although we had used an *eight-percent* inflation rate, the resulting dollar amount lost to inflation eroded his gross income by *eleven percent*. As I explained to Jack, inflation doesn't just cut into profits, but into the original capital as well. Essentially, Jack was losing eight percent of his starting capital each year, plus another 4.33 percent (prorated) of any gains throughout the year.

With a *Mercenary* mindset, Jack would have immediately realized that a ten-percent return on his mutual fund, and a 3.5 percent savings interest rate, were not enough to overcome the attack on his capital. The calculations proved that Jack needed to earn *twelve percent* returns on all his investments just to break even! And we hadn't factored in the other taxes he was paying. For example, Jack was also paying around $1,750 in annual property taxes and we estimated that he paid out at least $1,500 per year in state sales tax. These two items alone added three-percent more to Jack's tax bracket.

When I completed the calculations for Jack, he nearly lost his lunch. He could see that almost half of his income went up in smoke every year. I gave him a few moments to digest the bad news before hitting him with the kicker. "Do you know what else, Jack?" He glared at me. I continued, "When you die, the government will take up to half of your remaining capital and assets, even though they've already been taxed." Fortunately, I was beyond Jack's reach at the time or I might have been punched!

A few weeks later, I received an e-mail from Jack thanking me for solving the mystery of why he never seemed to make enough money to keep up with the rising cost of living in his state. He then related that, after showing our calculations to his wife, she had asked him (rhetorically, of course), "Do we live in a socialist country or something?"

As a capitalist, I was tempted to return a warning about Karl Marx's call for *a heavy progressive income tax* and *the elimination of all rights of inheritance.* But, I restrained myself and, instead, sent Jack the famous Will Rogers one-liner: "Just be glad you're **not** getting all the government you're paying for."

$1 Million after Taxes and Inflation

In school we learned about the *Seven Ancient Wonders of the World.* Of these *Wonders*, only one remains intact today: the Great Pyramids of Egypt. To the best of my recollection, my teachers never taught me about the **eighth** wonder of the world, which is related to, but even more powerful than, a pyramid: *compounded interest.* Throughout history, the secret of compounding has produced some of the greatest fortunes ever accumulated.

The simplest example of this power can be illustrated with two deals. The first deal offers to give you $10,000 in cash every day for thirty days; the second offers you one penny, doubled each day for thirty days. Which deal makes you the most cash? The first deal yields a total of $300,000. The second deal starts off very slowly, but reaches nearly $21,000 in 22 days, and nets a total of $5.36 Million a mere eight days later. The lesson here is that, once you have made an investment profit, you should immediately reinvest it, thereby compounding your returns - making interest on the interest as well as on your principle. Many investors spend their profits, but successful investors keep them working. An old saying sums it up: "Money makes money, and the money money makes money."

Compounding is just one of many weapons in *The Stock Market Mercenary's* arsenal, but - of course - it's not as simple as I have described. Why not? Taxes and inflation will eat away at your profits whether you compound them or not. Plus, if you can find an investment method that allows you to double your money every day for thirty days, let me know!

To further illustrate the power of compounding against the weapons of inflation and taxes, let us devise a hypothetical investment scenario and test it against the mathematics. The rules of this scenario are as follows:

- Your starting capital is $6,000, deposited as one lump sum.

- You will deposit an additional $500 per month, and continue this pattern through the end.

- You will reinvest all net profits, after capital gains taxes.

- The capital gains tax rate remains constant at 28 percent.

- The true inflation rate remains constant at 8 percent, and the prorated annual inflation on one year's worth of monthly deposits is 4.33 percent.[21]

- The gross profit earned each year on your working capital remains constant at an aggressive 25 percent per year (yes, such returns are possible!).

- Your goal is to build the total account to at least One Million Dollars.

The question is, using the above rules, how many years will it take to increase your account to $1 Million in inflation-adjusted dollars? The answer is: 29 years! Scenario 1 (Figure 2-3) below shows the year-by-year results and summarizes the entire plan.

Note that the Effective Annual Percentage Rate (APR) of this 29-year scenario is equivalent to having *no taxes*, *no inflation*, and a modest 10.72 percent profit each year on your capital. Therefore, to realize 10.72 percent APR in today's economy, you must earn 25 percent in gross annual profits. Now, I must point out that the final ("nominal") balance in your account after this scenario would actually be much higher than is shown; more like 1.7 Million dollars. But it would *spend* like $1 Million in *today's* dollars. The point of this exercise is to show the erosion of purchasing power and the cost of taxation, even while applying the secret of compounding to your plan. Of course, I could have just used a standard NPV (net present value) formula to achieve similar results, but I wanted you to see the "internals" of this Scenario.

An alarming result in the above scenario is the total cost of inflation. Note that, after 29 years, inflation will have cost you more than capital gains taxes. This fact confirms the conclusions of the CBO study quoted earlier in this chapter. Finally, note the effective "Combined Rate" of inflation and taxes. If Americans realized that their true "tax rate" was nearly 60 percent on long-term investments, the public outcry would be deafening.

---

[21] A $500 deposit at the start of the year will be cut by the full 8%. The next month's $500 will be cut by 11/12ths of the inflation rate, or 7.33%, then 10/12ths, and so on. The total cost of inflation on 12 months of such payments will be $260, which is 4.33% of the year's deposit total of $6,000.

Compounding Profits - Scenario 1 (Detail)

Year	Capital *	25% Profits	28% Taxes	8% Inflation	Balance
0	6,000	-	-	-	6,000
1	6,000	1,500	(420)	(480)	6,600
2	12,600	3,150	(882)	(788)	14,080
3	20,080	5,020	(1,406)	(1,386)	22,308
4	28,308	7,077	(1,982)	(2,045)	31,358
5	37,358	9,340	(2,615)	(2,769)	41,314
6	47,314	11,829	(3,312)	(3,565)	52,266
7	58,266	14,567	(4,079)	(4,441)	64,313
8	70,313	17,578	(4,922)	(5,405)	77,564
9	83,564	20,891	(5,849)	(6,465)	92,141
10	98,141	24,535	(6,870)	(7,631)	108,175
11	114,175	28,544	(7,992)	(8,914)	125,813
12	131,813	32,953	(9,227)	(10,325)	145,214
13	151,214	37,804	(10,585)	(11,877)	166,556
14	172,556	43,139	(12,079)	(13,584)	190,032
15	196,032	49,008	(13,722)	(15,463)	215,855
16	221,855	55,464	(15,530)	(17,528)	244,261
17	250,261	62,565	(17,518)	(19,801)	275,507
18	281,507	70,377	(19,706)	(22,301)	309,877
19	315,877	78,969	(22,111)	(25,050)	347,685
20	353,685	88,421	(24,758)	(28,075)	389,273
21	395,273	98,818	(27,669)	(31,402)	435,020
22	441,020	110,255	(30,871)	(35,062)	485,342
23	491,342	122,836	(34,394)	(39,087)	540,697
24	546,697	136,674	(38,269)	(43,516)	601,586
25	607,586	151,897	(42,531)	(48,387)	668,565
26	674,565	168,641	(47,219)	(53,745)	742,242
27	748,242	187,061	(52,377)	(59,639)	823,287
28	829,287	207,322	(58,050)	(66,123)	912,436
29	918,436	229,609	(64,291)	(73,255)	1,010,499

Compounding Profits - Scenario 1 (Summary)

Total Invested	Gross Profits	Total Taxes	Total Inflation	Final Result
$ 174,000	2,075,844	(581,236)	(658,109)	$1,010,499

Net Profits	Real Tax Rate	Inflation Rate	Combined Rate	Effective A.P.R.
836,499	28.0%	31.7%	59.7%	10.72%

FIGURE 2-3. (Scenario 1) The power of compounded profits: starting with $6,000 and adding $6,000 per year thereafter, in monthly increments. The Scenario assumes 25% gross annual profits, a 28% capital gains tax rate, and an 8% prorated inflation rate. * Capital amounts do not reflect the monthly deposits until the beginning of the following year - making the final result slightly more conservative.

If you are like me, you are curious to find out, using the same investment scenario, how many years it would take to reach $1 Million *without the deductions for taxes or inflation*. The answer is: just 16 years! In such a "perfect" world, your total investment would be a mere $96,000 over 16 years, but you would pocket $939,843 in profits. See Scenario 2 below (Figure 2-4) for the results.

Compounding Profits - Scenario 2 (Detail)

Year	Capital *	25% Profits	00% Taxes	0% Inflation	Balance
0	6,000	-	-	-	6,000
1	6,000	1,500	-	-	7,500
2	13,500	3,375	-	-	16,875
3	22,875	5,719	-	-	28,594
4	34,594	8,649	-	-	43,243
5	49,243	12,311	-	-	61,554
6	67,554	16,889	-	-	84,443
7	90,443	22,611	-	-	113,054
8	119,054	29,764	-	-	148,818
9	154,818	38,705	-	-	193,523
10	199,523	49,881	-	-	249,404
11	255,404	63,851	-	-	319,255
12	325,255	81,314	-	-	406,569
13	412,569	103,142	-	-	515,711
14	521,711	130,428	-	-	652,139
15	658,139	164,535	-	-	822,674
16	828,674	207,169	-	-	1,035,843

Compounding Profits - Scenario 2 (Summary)

Total Invested	Gross Profits	Total Taxes	Total Inflation	Final Result
$ 96,000	939,843	-	-	$1,035,843

Net Profits	Real Tax Rate	Inflation Rate	Combined Rate	Effective A.P.R.
939,843	0.0%	0.0%	0.0%	28.15%

FIGURE 2-4. (Scenario 2) The power of compounded profits: starting with $6,000 and adding $6,000 per year thereafter, in monthly increments. The Scenario assumes 25% gross annual profits, no capital gains taxes, and no inflation.

Finally, if you're like me (and apparently you are), you are curious about the annual returns required to achieve our $1 Million target, *within the same 16 years* as in Scenario 2, *with taxes and inflation applied*. Anticipating your curiosity, I ran Scenario 3 (Figure 2-5) just for fun.

Compounding Profits - Scenario 3 (Detail)

Year	Capital *	45.5% Profits	28% Taxes	8% Inflation	Balance
0	6,000	-	-	-	6,000
1	6,000	2,730	(764)	(480)	7,486
2	13,486	6,136	(1,718)	(859)	17,045
3	23,045	10,485	(2,936)	(1,624)	28,970
4	34,970	15,911	(4,455)	(2,578)	43,848
5	49,848	22,681	(6,351)	(3,768)	62,410
6	68,410	31,127	(8,716)	(5,253)	85,568
7	91,568	41,663	(11,666)	(7,105)	114,460
8	120,460	54,809	(15,347)	(9,417)	150,505
9	156,505	71,210	(19,939)	(12,300)	195,476
10	201,476	91,672	(25,668)	(15,898)	251,582
11	257,582	117,200	(32,816)	(20,387)	321,579
12	327,579	149,048	(41,733)	(25,986)	408,908
13	414,908	188,783	(52,859)	(32,973)	517,859
14	523,859	238,356	(66,740)	(41,689)	653,786
15	659,786	300,203	(84,057)	(52,563)	823,369
16	829,369	377,363	(105,662)	(66,130)	1,034,940

Compounding Profits - Scenario 3 (Summary)

Total Invested	Gross Profits	Total Taxes	Total Inflation	Final Result
$ 96,000	1,719,377	(481,427)	(299,010)	$1,034,940

Net Profits	Real Tax Rate	Inflation Rate	Combined Rate	Effective A.P.R.
938,940	28.0%	17.4%	45.4%	28.15%

FIGURE 2-5. (Scenario 3) The power of compounded profits: starting with $6,000 and adding $6,000 per year thereafter, in monthly increments. The Scenario assumes 45.5% gross annual profits, a 28% capital gains tax rate, and an 8% prorated inflation rate.

In this final Scenario, we see that the combined tax and inflation rate (45.4%) is almost equal to the gross annual profit rate. But since we only need 16 years to reach our goal, the overall effects of inflation are not as severe as in the first Scenario's 29-year model.

The real problem illustrated by these Scenarios is that the rate of return required to overcome the enemy's weapons is far higher than most people think. *No longer should an eight-percent - or even twelve-percent - return in a mutual fund or other investment be considered "reasonable" or "acceptable."* **Until inflation drops to *zero* and stays there, both our capital and our gains are in jeopardy.**

I've been challenged many times to suggest a way to eliminate inflation. Since a return to gold-backed dollars appears to be nowhere on our horizon, the next-best solution comes from none other than Warren Buffett:

I could eliminate inflation or reduce it very easily, if you had a constitutional amendment that said that no congressman or senator was eligible for reelection in a year in which the CPI increased [by more than] 3 percent.[22]

Buffett made that suggestion in 1985 when the country's money supply (M3) was at $3.03 Trillion. Since then, America's money supply has nearly **tripled**.[23]

Summary

If your goal is to increase your *real* wealth from this point forward, you must **1)** avoid dying, and **2)** develop an investment plan that can overcome inflation and taxes with enough left over to achieve your desired capital growth. Since most of us are mere mortals, it is my opinion that a strategy to accomplish **#2** is the way to go! But, you have barely started your *Stock Market Mercenary* training, and there are additional enemies lurking in the shadows and targeting your capital. To beat them, you must first know who (or what) they are, where they came from, how they operate, and what defensive measures are available.

---

[22] Warren Buffett, March 13, 1985. "Investing in Equity Markets," quoted in Columbia University Business School, transcript of a seminar, p.23. (the abbreviation, CPI, means "consumer price index")
[23] Federal Reserve, "H.6 Release" (January 15, 2003).

Chapter 3: The Market Manipulators

How Insiders and Institutions Eat the Stock Traders' Lunch.

Manipulation comes in many flavors. On a *macro* level, manipulation can affect an entire market sector, such as the airlines or the telecom industry; or the entire stock market in the case of an oil embargo or massive currency devaluation. On a *micro* level, manipulation can involve the influencing of the public's perception of an individual stock or mutual fund. On a *sub-micro* level, manipulation can occur when a broker scams individual traders out of their working capital through "churning,"[24] or by recommending stocks in which the broker has a conflict of interest, or by any one of dozens of techniques.

Before proceeding with this chapter, I must satisfy my legal counsel by reiterating *for the record*, my intent. As I stated on the "Legalese" page earlier in the book (just in cased you skipped it):

> Nothing in this book is intended to accuse specific corporate insiders or investment professionals of intentionally unethical or illegal practices. In most cases, the manipulations discussed herein are simply consequences of the existing capitalist system.

It can be demonstrated that the very freedoms guaranteed by capitalism also provide a haven for those with enough savvy to prey upon the weakest of market participants. The victims are usually the least informed, or the ones most influenced by emotional appeals to their greed or fear. While history proves that people fail to learn from history, successful stock traders - and *Stock Market Mercenaries* - are willing to learn from the mistakes of others.

This chapter will expose the extent to which stock traders are risking their capital when they engage in the trading of equities. In order to do this, I must discuss real events, with real people and companies; not just theories. While most of the actions these real people and companies allegedly have taken were motivated by the desire to profit, many shareholders - especially those who didn't do their homework - lost all or a part of their investments as a direct result.

Most of the data used to substantiate my conclusions is *public record*. For example, whenever a corporate insider or an institutional trader buys or sells a company's stock, it is reported to the Securities and Exchange Commission (SEC). Whenever a public company files a quarterly financial statement or makes any change to its public financial profile, the information is submitted to the SEC. Thus, every transaction that could affect the stock or its price is public record, and available to those with the time and patience to search for it on the SEC's website. In addition, we have access to information about public corporations from media reports, court

---

[24] Brokers "churn" an account by buying and selling more frequently than necessary in order to generate higher commissions.

records, government transcripts, and public statements by corporate executives on TV market shows.

Despite the presence of all this information, apparently, most of the public does not have the time or desire to investigate the companies they trade, leaving that chore to their stockbrokers or the market analysts on television. In my opinion, relying on a stockbroker's "research" is like letting a coyote manage the chicken coop. **No one but you has a stake in the loss of your capital.** Stockbrokers get paid whether you win or lose in the market. In order to protect yourself, you must understand how the "coyotes" run their business. My goal in this chapter is to help you "connect the dots" toward the formulation of effective defenses. Like the previous chapter, this one may make you a little angry. I hope so!

But, since you have chosen to be a *Stock Market Mercenary*, a brief look at some of capitalism's past should be helpful. It is easier to understand and, therefore, to overcome certain manipulations if one knows where such activities originated. This is especially true since most of today's market scams are simply variations of themes as old as the American Colonies.

Tricks as Old as Capitalism

The Dutch are credited with the invention of modern capitalism in the early seventeenth century. In fact, New York was first a Dutch settlement, called "Nieuw Amsterdam" in the 1620s. In order to protect its profitable trading posts from feared New England attacks, colony governor Peter Stuyvesant built a wooden wall at the shoreline, protecting a quarter-mile area today known as "Wall Street."

Dutch Tricks

Meanwhile, in the Netherlands, early techniques of stock trading and manipulation were born. According to financial historian, John Steele Gordon, in his book *The Great Game*,[25] the Dutch invented many of the modern market tricks, including (but not limited to):

- **Short selling** - selling stock you don't own in hopes of a fall in price. The mechanics are simple: you borrow shares from a broker to sell, then buy shares at a lower price later to replace the borrowed shares (also called "covering shorts"), and keep the profits. It is this trick from whence comes the old rhyme: "He who sells what isn't his'n, must buy it back or go to prison."[26]

- **Bear raids** - insiders conspire to sell a stock short until the outsiders panic and sell out their holdings, allowing the insiders to "cover" their short positions profitably.

- **Syndicates** - a group of insiders manipulate a stock price by buying and selling among themselves.

- **Cornering** - a person or syndicate secretly acquires the entire "floating" supply of a commodity or stock, thereby trapping the market into a "corner," and forcing everyone else to buy that commodity or stock at the perpetrator's price.

---

[25] John Steele Gordon, 1999. "The Great Game" (Scribner, New York, NY), p.23.
[26] Attributed to speculator, Daniel Drew, mid-1800s, but original authorship is unverified.

As we will see, most of the manipulations that occur in today's stock market are simply new versions of the above tricks. Add the modern media and the Internet to the fray, and we also witness the routine manipulation of public psychology.

One of the first major attempts to "corner" a market occurred in the Netherlands, in 1635, when prices of the "Childer" variety of tulips rose to astronomical levels (two bulbs went for the equivalent of 14 tons of cheese plus a new carriage, two gray horses, and harness). One trader finally realized that "speculation" simply *transfers* wealth, and does not actually *create* wealth, so he courageously began selling short. The "tulip crash" that followed was equaled only by the buying frenzy that had started the tulip craze weeks before.[27]

The *New York Stock and Exchange Board* was created in 1817, patterned after the then successful *Philadelphia Stock Exchange*. Rules were established to curtail wild speculation and manipulation schemes, but for every rule there is a loophole, and new schemes were hatched almost immediately.

Speculators have for years held a reputation of "illegitimacy" - considered by some to be parasites, feeding off the capitalist system and profiting from activities that produce no new wealth. However, one benefit of speculation is unmistakable: liquidity. Brokers love speculators because they trade frequently, providing endless sources of commissions, and they ensure that other traders always have a *Greater Fool* to sell to - a necessary evil, perhaps. The great British financier, Sir Ernest Cassel, at the turn of the twentieth century, put it in perspective:

> When I was young, people called me a gambler. As the scale of my operations increased, I became known as a speculator. Now I am called a banker. But I have been doing the same thing all the time.[28]

The Erie Railroad Squeeze

In the 1830s, the Erie Railroad was a model of how **not** to build a railroad. Essentially designed by politicians, the Erie linked two insignificant small towns between the shores of Lake Erie and the Hudson River, approximately 480 miles apart. The cost to build this line exceeded $23 million on an original estimate of just $10 million. As a result, the railroad continued to use Wall Street for further financing. Using "convertible bonds," which could be exchanged freely with stock, the Erie was soon used for every speculative trick in the book. The amount of money needed was too much for New York, so much of the supply of Erie bonds was sold in London, and then promptly forgotten about.

Along came speculator, Jacob Little, who in 1837 let it be known that he was selling Erie short. A small syndicate of New York brokers decided to corner the market on Erie stock and squeeze Little when he would later try to cover his short positions. The syndicate quietly bought every available share in the "float" (shares not inscribed with an owner's name but allowed to float amongst brokers), hoping to force Little to pay high prices for his folly.[29]

What the syndicate did not know was that Little had been secretly buying up convertible bonds in London, which he now used to exchange for stock to cover his short positions. The syndicate was left holding the bag, having to unload thousands of shares at a huge loss.

---

[27] Gordon, pp. 23,24.
[28] Edward Chancellor, 1999. "Devil Take the Hindmost: A History of Financial Speculation" (Farrar, Straus and Giroux, New York, NY), p. ix.
[29] Gordon, pp. 77,78.

Watered Stock

A recurring name in the early years of the stock market, especially in reference to scams and manipulation, was Daniel Drew. At one point, Drew was considered among the top twenty richest people in America. In one of his most infamous capers, Drew supposedly bought cattle from farmers outside of New York, and herded them to New York City for sale and butchering. The story goes that, the night before reaching New York, Drew gave the herd all the salt they could eat, and deprived them of water until they reached a stream the next morning, mere blocks from their final destination. The cattle, of course, rushed to the stream and gulped up far more than they would have under normal circumstances, increasing their weight considerably and the profits by which Drew benefited. The term "watered stock" has ever since been attributed to this sort of scam. Nowadays, however, that term is applied to a company's shares being issued in larger quantities than the paid-in capital would dictate.[30]

Out-speculating the Speculators

In the mid-1800s, Cornelius Vanderbilt (affectionately called the "Commodore") gained a reputation as a "white hat" speculator, meaning someone who traded honestly (hold that thought), shrewdly, and one who often captured the manipulators in their own traps. Of course, if the Commodore were alive today, I would hail him as a *Stock Market Mercenary*! Vanderbilt had established a reputation as one of the most efficient steamboat and railroad managers of his day, able to nurture profits from just about any suffering business. Take the New York and Harlem Railroad, known as "The Harlem," for instance.

In 1863, The Harlem was losing money due to poor management. In fact, the *New York Herald* reported that, "…of all the railroad shares dealt in, the Harlem probably possesses the least intrinsic value."[31] But Vanderbilt recognized the potential to turn the railroad into a profitable concern. During that era, local city councils made today's political "pork" spending and corruption look like child's play, and Vanderbilt knew well how to "use" such greedy politicians. The Commodore began to accumulate Harlem stock, knowing that the railroad was about to be granted the rights by the city council to a streetcar franchise up Broadway, the busiest thoroughfare. Such consideration, of course, was well paid for by the existing Harlem directors, and many council members were also buying up Harlem stock. Why is this important? Because earlier the same council had voted to restrict the Harlem's "dirty and dangerous" rail rights, making the railroad's stock even less desirable, thus allowing council members to buy it cheap.

The major speculators and brokers on the Street were selling the Harlem short, while Vanderbilt openly bought every Harlem share in sight. These "bears" sold so much stock that the price tumbled to the low $50s by April 23rd, the day the council passed the Broadway franchise bill. On May 19th, the price had risen to $116^{5/8}$ but then the short selling began, perpetrated by none other than Daniel Drew, a member of the Harlem's board of directors.

Vanderbilt continued to buy despite the downward pressure. Then, on June 25th, the bottom fell out when the council rescinded the Broadway streetcar franchise. The price dropped to 72 by the close of the day and the bears were certain they had brought down the Commodore. Instead,

---

[30] Gordon, pp. 82,83.
[31] New York Herald, March 25, 1863.

the next day, the price rose back to 97, and the next day, 106. The short sellers, it seems, had shorted (borrowed) more shares than existed, because Vanderbilt had bought more than the majority of all stock in the Harlem. Now, the bears had to buy at high prices from Vanderbilt in order to replace the borrowed shares they had shorted. Thus, Vanderbilt had bested the best speculators on Wall Street.[32]

Fast-forward to the Roaring 20s.

The Graham Straddle

As I have indicated, not all market manipulation is necessarily "bad," especially if you're the manipulator. Sometimes one need only take advantage of the *apparent* manipulations of others. That's what Benjamin Grossbaum, a.k.a., Benjamin Graham,[33] did by being observant and by doing his homework. A scholarly type, Graham learned to read in at least six languages, including Latin and Greek. More importantly, Graham gained a reputation for being able to spot opportunities within the financial statements of companies.

For example, in the early 1920s Graham spotted what is now called a "straddle" opportunity (allowing one to play both ends of the market). He noticed that Du Pont share prices were virtually the same as General Motors (GM) prices, even though Du Pont, at the time, was a major shareholder of GM as well as other large companies. Graham reasoned that the market was either undervaluing Du Pont or overvaluing GM. It didn't matter to him. He bought a large amount of Du Pont shares and sold short an equal amount of GM shares, and then just waited.

It took awhile, but the market recognized the discrepancy and sent Du Pont prices up sharply while keeping GM relatively flat. Graham promptly covered his GM short position at break-even while making a bundle on the Du Pont shares. If the opposite price movements had occurred, Graham would have made money as well.[34] Today, the "Graham Straddle" is used all the time to take advantage of apparent discrepancies between related stocks, or to "hedge" investments with opposing trades, "just in case." Like the Commodore, I consider Graham to have been a *Stock Market Mercenary*. Some of today's top investors, including Warren Buffett, have closely followed the investment philosophy of Benjamin Graham.

Now that we have laid the historical foundation for market manipulation, both good and bad, it is time to expose the 21st Century's variations - from cases that will seem familiar to many of you, especially if you lost money in the "Technology Bubble" of 2000.

Modern Tricks: The Technology Bubble

It could be argued that, by the late twentieth century, government and the stock exchanges had tightened the reins on market manipulation through better enforcement of regulations and more stringent accounting practices. Like I said, it could be argued - but only a little. More and more, it seems, the front pages expose insider swindles that make some of the early "cornering" schemes look honorable. For example, take the industry in which I have spent over half of my life: Technologies.

---

[32] Gordon, pp. 102-104.

[33] With America's entry into World War I in 1917, those with German-sounding names tended to attract scorn, causing a flurry of name changes.

[34] Gordon, p. 256.

During the thirteen-month period of March 10, 2000 through April 6, 2001, the NASDAQ[35] alone, with it's predominant membership of high-technology and "dot-com" companies, plummeted from a total value of $7.6 trillion to a mere $2.4 trillion. According to Martin D. Weiss, PhD, chairman of Weiss Ratings, Inc., during this period, investors (mostly the non-professional public) lost $5.2 trillion, or "…more than was lost in the worst crashes of all recorded history, the equivalent of nearly half the entire gross domestic product of the most powerful economy in the world."[36]

An interesting fact is that, *before the decline, the tech-stocks' average price-to-earnings* (P/E) *ratio*[37] *exceeded* **740-to-1**,[38] *yet these stocks were highly touted and recommended on every form of market media available.*

Of course, *during* the decline of the market, corporate insiders (officers and directors) and institutional investors (mutual funds, banks, insurance companies, pension funds, etc.) lost very little money. How was this possible? In my opinion, the answer is simple: **the insiders knew the truth, and knew it in advance, while the uninformed public was actually hyped into buying at the top, allowing the insiders to "dump" their shares at high prices into the hands of the "sheeple."**[39]

I can hear you saying, "OK, Dan, now you've gone too far. You're generalizing, oversimplifying, and making a serious charge against a well-regulated industry." Let me respond by saying that, first, I am *indeed* generalizing, since I believe the entire network of corporate insiders, institutions, brokers, market analysts, market journals, and TV market commentators were willing, or unwitting, accomplices in this scheme. Second, I *am* oversimplifying, because it needs to be said in simple terms. And, third, my charge is *definitely* serious because the industry is certainly *not* sufficiently "well-regulated," although the government has tightened up *some* corporate accounting regulations of late.

The evidence that the stock-trading public was the victim of a major fleecing is not hard to find. The Securities and Exchange Commission is rife with the financial filings, insider trading notices, IPOs (initial public offerings), investigative reports, and bankruptcy notices that were generated before, during and after the "technology bubble." *Within those SEC filings, the news headlines, and the charts of the affected companies, are the numbers that prove the case.*[40]

The SEC has known for years that manipulation exists. For example, here is a warning from former SEC Chairman, Arthur Levitt, made during an address in 1998, prior to the peak of the "bubble":

> Increasingly, I have become concerned that the motivation to meet Wall Street earnings expectations may be overriding common-sense business practices. Too many corporate managers, auditors, and analysts are participants in a game of nods and winks. In the zeal to satisfy consensus earnings estimates and project a smooth earnings path, wishful thinking may be winning the day over faithful

---

[35] National Association of Securities Dealers. Apparently, the "AQ" was added for marketing purposes.
[36] Martin D. Weiss, PhD, 2002. "The Ultimate Safe Money Guide" (John Wiley & Sons, Inc., New York, NY), p. 3. [Copyright © 2002 Martin D. Weiss, Ph.D. This material is used by permission of John Wiley & Sons, Inc.]
[37] Price-to-earnings ratio is calculated by dividing the per-share sales price by the per-share net earnings of a company. The lower the ratio, the more financially healthy a company is considered to be. For example, Warren Buffett will rarely buy a company whose P/E ratio exceeds 10.
[38] NASDAQ Historical Archives (www.nasdaq.com)
[39] Sheeple: People who are herded like sheep to the slaughter.
[40] SEC: www.sec.gov

representation. ...As a result, I fear that we are witnessing an erosion in the quality of earnings, and therefore, the quality of financial reporting. Managing may be giving way to manipulation; integrity may be losing out to illusion.[41]

Sadly, Levitt's warning went unheeded. It took the Enron and Global Crossing fiascos, in which thousands of employees, and millions of shareholders, lost their equity to return the country's focus to the importance of *truth* in financial reporting. Notice that I said that the country's *focus* is on truth, not that truth is yet fully delivered. Meanwhile, back in 1999, the Priceline.com story was heating up, and truth was just "collateral damage."

The Priceline.com Saga

The story of Priceline.com is typical of the companies caught in the Tech Bubble of 2000. It is also tragic if you were an "outsider" who bought Priceline stock. Checking the archives of the top twenty brokerage firms, we find that nearly all, including Morgan Stanley Dean Witter, in the spring of 1999, gave Priceline.com a positive rating of "strong buy" or "outperform." These ratings were published in market journals, broadcast on TV market shows, and circulated all over the Internet. I remember watching CNBC's *SquawkBox™* show before the opening of each trading day, witnessing an endless parade of analysts and brokers tout the merits of Priceline.com, Amazon.com, and countless other Web stocks. On "Cinco de Mayo," 1999, *Priceline had reached $152 per share even though it had not made a dime of profit.* Yet, with 225 million shares outstanding, Priceline had been "valued" by the market at $34.2 billion, despite the company having no actual "product" to sell. The media's "story" was that Priceline was "a quintessential virtual business model" - a virtual online clearinghouse for unsold, low-cost airline seats and hotel rooms.

I remember asking anyone who would listen why they would buy a company that had never shown a profit, had little chance of ever doing so, and produced no real "product" of its own. The typical answer was, "Priceline is a *hot* stock." At the time, I had calculated a hypothetical P/E ratio, based upon Priceline earning just *one-penny* per share in profit, at 15,200-to-1. In other words, if you had bought all 225 million shares at $152 per share, at the rate of one-penny per share in profits per year, *it would have taken you 15,200 years just to break-even!* Since the company was, in reality, hopelessly in the red, the true P/E was stratospheric. Yet everyone was buying, and, it seemed, nobody in the media had anything negative to say about the stock.

From its public offering in '99, Priceline had launched an aggressive marketing campaign using celebrities and clever TV commercials to advertise for business, while brokers, analysts, and the market media continued to hype its stock. Among the SEC insider filings, I noticed that one company, *Vulcan Ventures Inc.* (a.k.a., *Vulcan Inc*), had been one of the early investors who wisely bought the stock before the public feeding frenzy. As it turns out, Vulcan was owned by Microsoft co-founder, Paul G. Allen. I don't know why I zeroed in on this particular insider. Perhaps it was because I was a fan of the *Star Trek™* series, or that one of its stars (William Shatner) was Priceline's spokesman, or that "Vulcan" was a species known for its logic and control over emotions (sounds like a *Stock Market Mercenary!*).

The following year, curious as to why the analysts and TV commentators were again hyping the stock, I visited the SEC website to read Priceline's latest financial statement. The first thing

---

[41] Arthur Levitt, September 28, 1998. "SEC Chairman Arthur Levitt, Concerned That the Quality of Corporate Financial Reporting Is Eroding, Announces Action Plan to Remedy Problem" (www.sec.gov/news/press/pressarchive/1998/98-95.txt).

that caught my eye was the enormous amount of cash the company had reported it was circulating, in stark contrast to the company's assets. The trend only got worse as the year progressed. By December 31, 2000, Priceline.com's *cash-to-assets ratio* (**[net income - net cash] ÷ total assets**), or what I call the *truth ratio*, was over 40 percent. To be reasonably assured that a company is honestly reporting earnings and cash-flow, and not attempting to hide any bad news, the *truth ratio* should be *under* 10 percent, but is even "safer" if under *four*-percent. At the end of that year, the Priceline situation was as follows (Figure 3-1):[42]

Priceline.com 4th Qtr, December 31, 2000	
Net Income	(105,135,000)
less Net Cash	(18,688,000)
[use absolute value] equals	86,447,000
divided by Total Assets	195,078,000
equals the "Truth Ratio"	44.31%
Source: SEC/Edgar Online	

FIGURE 3-1. Calculation of Priceline.com's "Truth Ratio" as of 4th quarter 2000.

When Priceline went public on March 31, 1999, the media-hyped stock opened at $75.25 per share, then more than doubled to $165 by April 30th. Support for the stock immediately began to disappear as the insiders started to sell their shares. Figure 3-2 illustrates the Priceline story. In the waning months of 1999, the stock had already plummeted to the $50's. The media hype began anew in early-March 2000, which briefly rallied the stock back to $90 and above, but alas, still no profits, still no support. By late spring, according to the SEC's insider trading reports, most of the institutional investors and corporate insiders had already divested their shares. **Obviously, since all the big players were selling - not buying - there could only be one group of stock traders who were buying - not selling: the public.**

Interestingly, Vulcan was one of the few insiders who had stayed with the stock even as it tumbled, until the price reached $49 (during extended hours trading), on June 1, 2000, selling 1.6 million shares for over $79 million.[43] This sale was public record, but, the original purchase price was not (pre-IPO, apparently), thus we do not know if Vulcan, by waiting, made or lost money on those shares. Earlier filings had shown that Vulcan - at one time - reported ownership of over 9 million shares, so it is "Vulcan logic" that the other 7.4 million shares were sold earlier at even better prices.

Meanwhile, other insiders were dumping their shares, including Chairman Richard S. Braddock ($38.8 million), Delta Air Lines Inc. ($512 million), Jay S. Walker ($374 million), Executive VP Timothy Brier ($8 million), and Senior VP Thomas D'Angelo ($4.7 million). In the case of the officers, and Delta Air Lines, the exercising of options at prices ranging from 80-cents to $2.97 per share, was the extent of their "risk." What a deal! Buy - as Chairman

---

[42] SEC/Edgar Online.
[43] SEC/Edgar Online Insider Trading

Braddock did - 96,500 shares on May 17 and 18, 2000, via exercise of option at 80-cents, then immediately sell those shares to the public at an average price of $51.59, receiving about $4,978,000.[44]

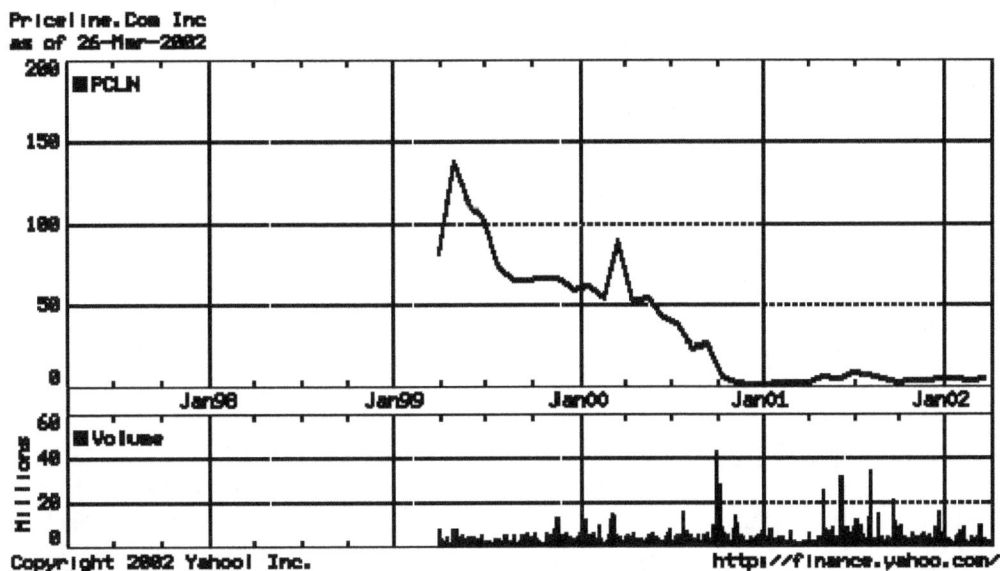

FIGURE 3-2. Lifetime price history of Priceline.com (PCLN) as of March 26, 2002.
[Reproduced with permission of Yahoo! Inc. © 2003 by Yahoo! Inc. YAHOO! and the YAHOO! logo are trademarks of Yahoo! Inc.]

The SEC/Edgar.com entries for Priceline, (see Figure 3-3) documents Braddock's transactions as described, as well as Vulcan's sale. These activities are just a few from among thousands captured on dozens of dot-coms during the same period.

Were these transactions illegal? No. Am I picking on these entities to build a case for "class envy?" Again, no. It is every red-blooded capitalist's dream to be able to make these exact kinds of stock deals. The issue is that, being insiders with access to the financial statements and internal strategies of the company, they **had to know** that Priceline.com was operating on a failed business model, and that the company's cash-to-assets ratio was at a *fatal* level. Whether you believe the previous sentence or not, the facts are irrefutable: **Priceline.com's insiders dumped their shares in the midst of a media- and broker-hyped feeding frenzy, while the buyers - the public - bought high and lost over $30 billion of their Priceline.com equity.**

On December 27, 2000, just 21 months after its opening, Priceline shares hit a low of $1.06, representing a loss of 99.4 percent of its value from the recorded high, and a loss of 98.6 percent from its opening price. Public records show the insiders selling at, or near the highs, and buying (exercising options) at pennies on the dollar, or at low, pre-IPO prices. The public, unfortunately, did the opposite. And, not being insiders, the public had no opportunity to own 80-cent options.

This situation begs the question: What force in this universe could possibly have induced millions of individual "outsider" public stock traders to buy Priceline shares when they did - at the exact moment when the insiders needed to dump their shares at substantially profitable prices? Further, what force could have induced the public to buy this story *twice* - once in 1999 and again in the spring of 2000? Could these millions of stock traders **all** have been stupid? **Or did they all receive the wrong advice?** Is it possible that millions of people suddenly picked up

---

[44] SEC/Edgar Online Insider Trading

the phone, or logged into the Internet, and collectively decided that they should all buy Priceline shares at the top, without a single bit of encouragement from anyone?

2000-05-17	BRADDOCK, RICHARD S.	Chairman	500,000	Planned Sale (Estimated proceeds of $29,000,000)
2000-05-17 - 2000-05-18	BRADDOCK, RICHARD S.	Chairman	96,500	Option Exercise at $0.80 per share. (Cost of $77,200)
2000-05-17 - 2000-05-18	BRADDOCK, RICHARD S.	Chairman	*96,500	Sale at $50.671 - $52.5 per share. (Proceeds of about
2000-06-05	BRADDOCK, RICHARD S.	Chairman	*48,150	Sale at $50.282 per share. (Proceeds of $2,421,078)
2000-08-06 - 2000-08-15	BRADDOCK, RICHARD S.	Chairman	100,000	100,000 Option Exercise at $0.80 per share. (Cost of
2000-08-15 - 2000-08-16	BRADDOCK, RICHARD S.	Chairman	*100,000	Sale at $25.321 - $25.524 per share. (Proceeds of about
2000-06-01	VULCAN VENTURES INC.		1,620,000	Planned Sale (Estimated proceeds of $79,380,000)

FIGURE 3-3. Insider trading reports. Source: SEC/Edgar-Online.com
* shareholder used a trust or other instrument for the transaction

The evidence is clear, by the insiders' own SEC-recorded transactions, by the recorded broadcasts of the morning market TV shows, by the printed market journals, and by the published "buy" and "strong buy" ratings of most of the brokerages, that the public psychology was hyped into wanting that "hot" Priceline stock. Think about this: How could competing brokers, competing TV shows, and competing publications all be singing the same tune - touting the same stock at the same time - without this dance being choreographed? Is this just the way the game is played - "the luck of the dice?" - or are the public stock traders simply *raw materials* in an elaborate scam?

One more pattern to consider, before we see further evidence. In our Priceline.com story, did you notice that the truly successful investors - the major shareholders and insiders - bought their shares cheap when the public didn't want them (or didn't know about them), and sold their shares "dear" when the public "dearly" wanted them? Remember Hetty Green's advice in Chapter 1? No? Go back and re-read it now. (I'll wait!)

Although it is clear that mass manipulation is afoot, the public continues to buy high and sell low, and the media continues to tout stocks whose rallies are finished, or nearly finished. This is chronically followed by advice to "take your losses" at some scientifically formulated level, almost always below the purchase price. While I concede that there are a few lone, contrarian voices in the media, they are rare exceptions. Those with *bad* advice, rule.

Unfortunately, during the Tech Bubble, this pattern of behavior was repeated many times with hundreds of high-flying firms, adding up to the five-plus trillion dollar rip-off of the public's investment capital. I have included for your perusal a few more charts of companies whose fortunes were made and lost during the technology bubble. Notice the similarities to the Priceline.com pattern.

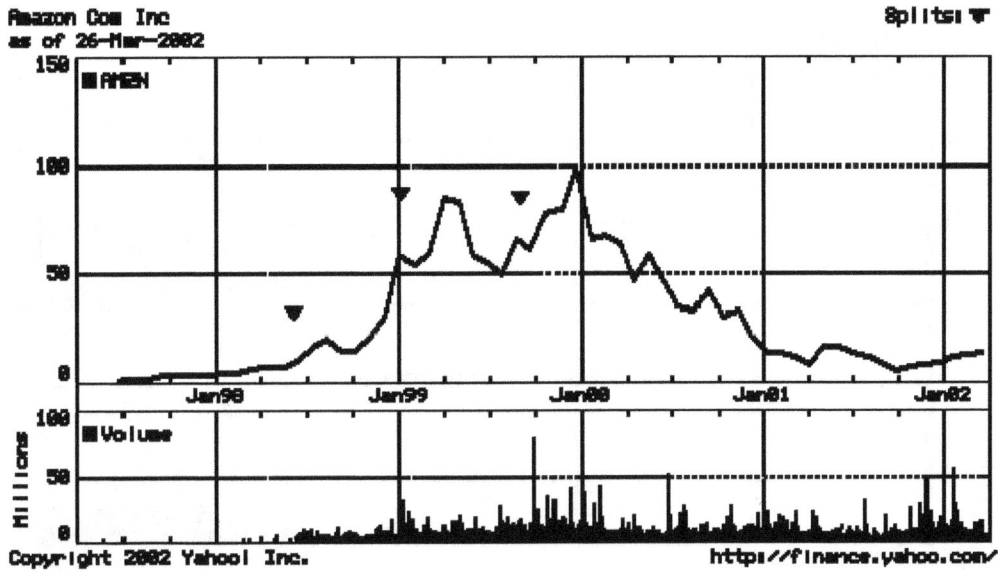

FIGURE 3-4. Lifetime split-adjusted price history of Amazon.com (AMZN) as of March 26, 2002. [Reproduced with permission of Yahoo! Inc. © 2003 by Yahoo! Inc. YAHOO! and the YAHOO! logo are trademarks of Yahoo! Inc.]

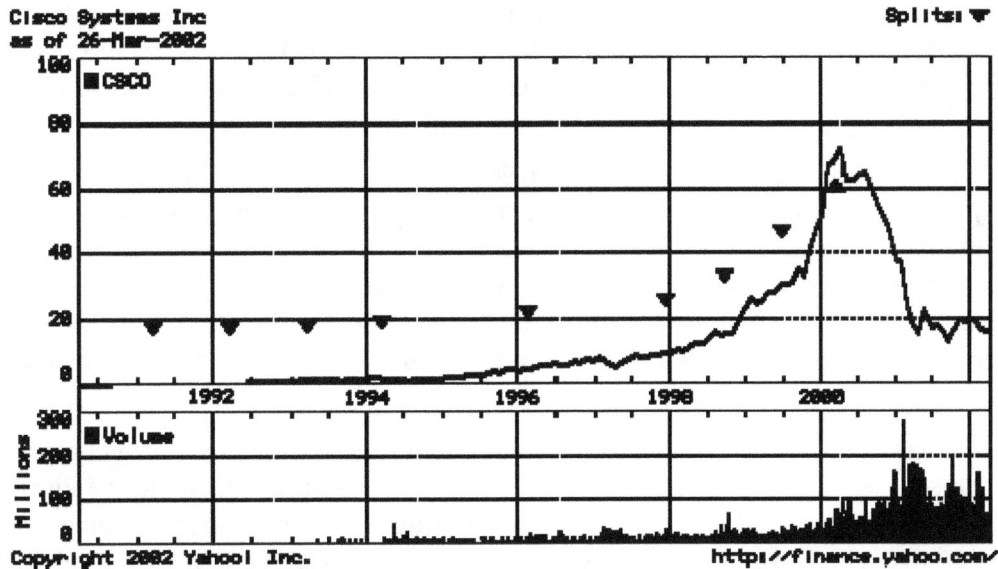

FIGURE 3-5. Lifetime split-adjusted price history of Cisco Systems (CSCO) as of March 26, 2002. [Reproduced with permission of Yahoo! Inc. © 2003 by Yahoo! Inc. YAHOO! and the YAHOO! logo are trademarks of Yahoo! Inc.]

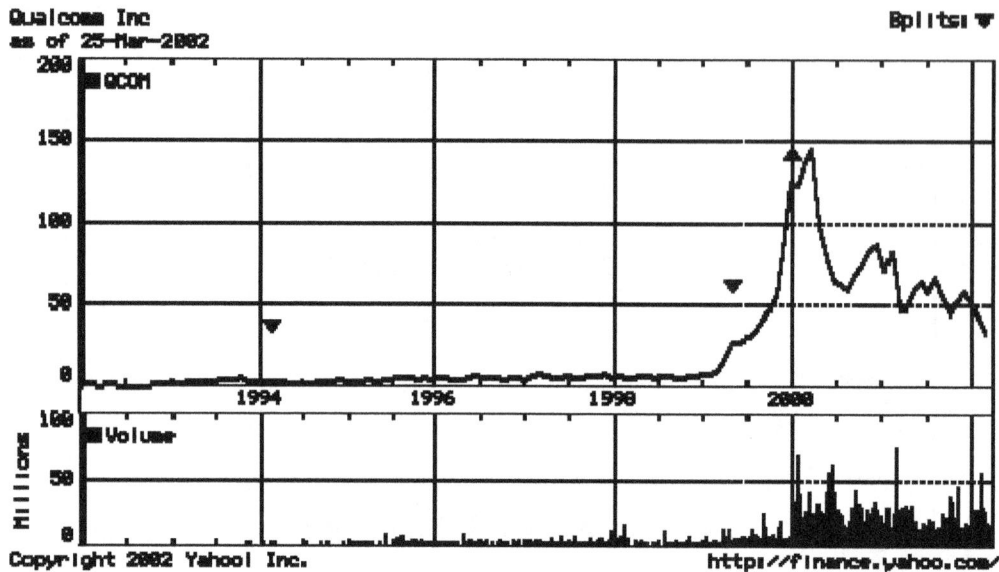

FIGURE 3-6. Lifetime split-adjusted price history of Qualcomm (QCOM) as of March 25, 2002. [Reproduced with permission of Yahoo! Inc. © 2003 by Yahoo! Inc. YAHOO! and the YAHOO! logo are trademarks of Yahoo! Inc.]

In most of these charts, and hundreds like them, we see that a long period of "normal" gradual, sideways growth is interrupted by a brief exponential rise, followed by a sharp ("falling knife") decline, followed by a long gradual sideways decline or flat consolidation period. Also note that the trading volumes (bottom chart under the price chart) during the spikes and long declines are much higher than in the periods before and after the "bubble."

This period of high volume during high stock prices is called "distribution," when the major investors are dumping their shares, literally "distributing" them to the uninformed (or gullible) public. How do we know this? It's easy: *for every buyer, there must be a seller*. **Dramatically higher-than-average volumes indicate major movements of large blocks of shares each day over a sustained period. The only entities able to trade large enough quantities of shares to cause these volume spikes - and to thus move the market - are insiders and institutional investors.**

Once all shares have been transferred into the public's hands, support for a company's stock vanishes, causing a free-fall in the stock's price, until it hits bottom. How do we know that the insiders and institutions actually dump their shares during this time period? Fortunately, the SEC takes care of that chore for us, and reports the trading activities of insiders and institutions regularly. If the public really wanted to know the truth, they could find it - for free - on the Internet. Apparently, the public does not feel the need to challenge the hype they are fed by the investment professionals who advise them.

The pattern I have described can be demonstrated repeatedly on company after company - in fact, the majority of the nearly 10,000 public firms in the U.S. show a frighteningly similar pattern on their long-term charts, some more than once during their lifetimes. In other words, it is a recurring pattern of manipulation that is repeated every five to eight years. Keep this pattern in mind for now - it is one that *Stock Market Mercenaries* can use to their advantage!

Note that the *price pattern* followed by these companies is similar. I did **not** say that the companies *themselves* were *causing* these patterns. Institutional investors, for example, are primarily opportunists with the ability to control large blocks of shares and to, thus, move the price up or down at will. These *cornering* and/or *syndicate* actions allow them to virtually guarantee their desired profit. In most cases, institutional investors do not interfere with the internal strategies of the companies. This was confirmed by a recent PricewaterhouseCoopers (PWC) Management Barometer survey of the top 120 corporations. PWC found that "Institutional investors hold more than 60 per cent of shares in most large, multinational companies," but also discovered that these investors rarely attempted to influence company strategies to any significant degree.[45] Actually, this is a logical situation. **If you can control the price of the stock, it matters little whether you control the company's management.**

Further evidence of the potential for *cornering* and *syndicate* manipulation can be found through laborious tallying of institutional and insider ownership records filed with the SEC. Best estimates indicate that, based on a snapshot of SEC raw data, **at the end of October 2002, approximately 75 investors held more than thirty-five percent (35%) of all the outstanding shares traded at the major stock exchanges in the United States.**[46] Hypothetically (of course), if these investors decided to either buy-up or sell-out a particular stock, is it even remotely possible that the resulting price action of that stock would move dramatically upward or downward, respectively?

The Great Stock Market Scam

As we have seen, Priceline.com was not the only company to follow the pattern of over-hype, feeding frenzy, insider dumping, and public losses. During the same period, names such as Amazon.com (87.6% loss), Proctor & Gamble (56% loss), Cisco (57% loss), Oracle (53% loss), and about 2,500 others, dropped like lemmings over a cliff. Once the panic started, even the companies with perfect accounting practices and no manipulation tactics were punished by the public in their haste to leave the stock market.

Dr. Weiss, in his excellent and timely book, *The Ultimate Safe Money Guide*, calls this period "The Great Stock Market Scam" and offers the following retrospection:

> A key cause was the companies' earnings, which turned out to be far lower than most everyone expected. Some companies couldn't claim a penny in earnings. Others couldn't even claim a penny in **sales**. But nearly all continued to brag about great results and get Wall Street's best ratings until virtually the bitter end. ... Their ubiquitous tool: **misinformation**.[47]

Dr. Weiss's staff performed a study of over 6,000 U.S. companies, comparing their reported earnings with their *actual* cash flows from operations. Such comparisons usually show a reasonable synchronization between the two. Instead, Weiss found that *thirty-one percent* (31%) showed marked discrepancies, leading him to suspect earnings manipulations (legal or illegal).[48]

Since earnings data is the single most important piece of information to "value investors," or "fundamentalists" (more on this later), it should come as no surprise that earnings information is

---

[45] PricewaterhouseCoopers Management Barometer, April 4, 2002. "Large Institutional Investors, Though Major Shareholders, Have Limited Influence on Corporate Strategy, PricewaterhouseCoopers Finds" (www.barometersurveys.com)
[46] SEC institutional and insider filings. (www.sec.gov) Obviously, ownership figures will vary on a daily basis as institutions and insiders buy and sell their shares.
[47] Weiss, p. 3. [emphasis his]
[48] Weiss, p. 5.

so often manipulated or distorted by company officials who are responsible for certifying the quarterly financials.

Dr. Weiss offers the answer to the question, "What is their motive?"

> The officials of America's corporations can get up to 90 percent of their compensation in stock and stock options. So they have everything to gain by putting out information that will boost the value of their own investments in the company.[49]

For example, in 2002, AOL's Steve Case earned a little over $1 million in salary, having already received over $158 million in stock and stock options in 1998. Intel Corporation's Craig Barrett earned around $2.6 million in salary, plus more than $114 million in stock and options. Disney's Michael Eisner earned $5.7 million plus around $569 million in stock and options. The list goes on and on.[50] The motivations of corporate officers should be readily apparent.

But we have barely scratched the surface. No study of stock market manipulation would be complete without the stories of Enron and Global Crossing!

Enron

Just say the word, "Enron," and people nod their heads in total agreement. Usually, no further discussion is needed. Enron has almost become a euphemism for any corporation that scams its shareholders or deprives its employees of their retirement accounts. What is missing from most discussions about Enron is the level and sophistication of their manipulations of the public, their employees, the accounting community, the SEC, and the federal courts. You see, Enron wasn't just an oil and gas energy trading company. In fact, the sale of oil and gas products was a *minor* part of Enron's business. Let me summarize the Enron story, condensed from over a year's worth of media coverage, both in print and on the air.

Enron's business model appears to have been *designed* to manipulate the system, to prey upon the uninformed (sound familiar?). For example, if your company had a financial statement that showed no debts, an investor reading the balance sheet would see an abundance of assets and a high margin of equity. That's exactly what the public saw, and they predictably responded by buying up Enron's shares. In fact, Enron had transferred their debts to offshore partnerships (of dubious origin). Profits looked very good to the public, the analysts, and the media alike, and Enron's stock prices soared to unprecedented levels. Once the stock prices hit $100 and above (way above), the insiders began exercising their options, selling their stock and pocketing hundreds of millions of dollars. (See Figure 3-7.)

Then, the public was informed about those hidden, unreported offshore debts, and Enron's stock price fell like a rock. In fact, the price dropped to well below the previous historical lows, so, guess what? You guessed right! The insiders started buying up those shares again at much lower prices than before. So far, the scheme sounds much like the other corporations caught in the technology bubble. Just build up the stock prices artificially using leverage, dump the shares on the public, leak some bad news, default the company, the public panics and sells out at a loss, wait for the price to hit new lows, and buy up the company again. Simple, right?

---

[49] Weiss, pp. 5-6.
[50] Yahoo! Finance, Company Profile Data.

ENRNQ (Enron) 10-Year view

FIGURE 3-7. 10-year split-adjusted price history of Enron (ENRNQ). [Reproduced with permission of Larkin Industries, Inc. © 2003 by LarkinSoft. LarkinSoft is a trademark of Larkin Industries, Inc.]

But the Enron manipulators weren't finished. Not only did they buy back their company cheaply, they still retained its assets. The Arthur Andersen accounting scandal that followed, and additional revelations from employee whistleblowers, sent Enron to Bankruptcy court. But remember, I said earlier that Enron was "sophisticated." The insiders used their Chapter 11 protection to split the company into multiple corporate entities, essentially allowing them to further hide or profit from the company's assets. For example, one of Enron's partners, UBS Warburg, was "rewarded" by the U.S. Bankruptcy Court with over $100 Billion in Enron assets, without the burden of those pesky liabilities.[51]

The bottom line was that Enron insiders got to keep the elevator while the creditors and stockholders got the shaft. As of this writing, SEC investigators are still trying to unravel the Enron story, and may never uncover just how "sophisticated" the insiders were.

Global Crossing and the Telecom Meltdown

We've seen that the technology bubble was not limited to Internet companies and information technology giants. Global Crossing went public in mid-1998, when there appeared to be no limit to the Internet explosion. The demand for global Web "data traffic" was touted by the company almost daily in the media, and the stock rallied from its $12 IPO price to the mid-$60s (split adjusted) in less than a year.

The early investors began selling in the spring of 1999, sending the price back down to $20 in late-summer. According to SEC filings, many of the insiders and institutions who made killings during Global Crossing's IPO rally, bought back in through the Fall of 1999. The media

---

[51] Washington Post, January 22, 2002; "Enron Raised Funds In Private Offering" (www.washingtonpost.com/wp-dyn/articles/A15912-2002Jan21.html)

blitz that followed through the holidays created a public stampede to buy the shares, which the insiders were more than happy to distribute - again. By March 2000, the high almost reached the stock's previous record. (See Figure 3-8.) As with the rest of the technology sector, Global Crossing suffered a free-fall to the mid $20s, finally capitulating to *one-penny* in early-2002.

FIGURE 3-8. 5-year split-adjusted price history of Global Crossing (GBLXQ).
[Reproduced with permission of Larkin Industries, Inc. © 2003 by LarkinSoft. LarkinSoft is a trademark of Larkin Industries, Inc.]

Global Crossing boasted a robust broadband network, for both voice and data transmissions, linking 200 cities in 27 countries. But, the company stood accused of manipulating its financial statements to appear profitable when it was deeply in the red. Like Enron, Global Crossing used Arthur Andersen LLP as its accountant and management consulting service. Many critics accused Global Crossing of holding mostly worthless assets while publicly reporting a huge potential demand for its broadband capacity and over $22 billion in assets. In January, 2002, the company filed Chapter 11, becoming the fourth largest bankruptcy in U.S. history.

During the first hearing by the House Financial Services Committee on Thursday, March 21, 2002, Representative Felix Grucci (R-N.Y.) characterized Global Crossing's exaggeration of its financial position as being motivated by "absolute, unfettered greed." As the hearing continued and the Committee realized that Global Crossing executives were not going to cooperate, Gucci expressed frustration that they would "not tell the truth, when asked ... and feel no shame or sense of guilt."[52]

The testimony of Global Crossing execs was contradicted by whistle-blower and former vice president of finance, Roy Olofson, who had written a five-page letter detailing the company's

---

[52] Shihoko Goto, Friday, March 22, 2002. "Global Crossing Similar to Enron" (United Press International)

deceptive accounting practices, including deliberately inflated revenue and cash flow figures to sweeten investors' perceptions of its stock value.[53]

According to the Committee's press release, Global Crossing's demise meant the loss of 9,000 jobs, the closure of 71 offices and resulted in "a meltdown in the value of the employees' 401(k) plans as the stock fell from a high of $64 a share to 30 cents before the company filed for bankruptcy."[54]

The apparent corruption, manipulation and insider trading did not end at the company's doors, but allegedly included Asia Global Crossing, Arthur Andersen LLP, some prominent state and national politicians,[55] many union leaders,[56] the chairman of the Democratic National Committee, the Chinese government (through surrogate companies such as Hutchison Whampoa Ltd.), and many others. Among the casualties were thousands of employees who lost their jobs and their retirement savings, along with millions of public shareholders. Global Crossing had even imposed a stock-trading blackout period during October of 2001, preventing employees from selling their shares, while chairman Gary Winnick managed to sell his shares worth in excess of $700 million, according to SEC records.

In fact, the House Committee noted that top Global Crossing executives sold over $1.3 billion in company stock from 1999 through 2001, and the company made last-minute pre-bankruptcy lump-sum executive pension payouts totaling $15 million. The Committee added, "The company also moved up its last payday by a week, so executives and others still employed could get paid before the company declared bankruptcy, while severance checks to employees already laid off weren't paid or bounced."[57]

What Enron was to the energy business, Global Crossing was to the telecom industry, according to Scott Cleland, founder and CEO of the Precursor Group®, an independent research company, who also testified before the House Committee on Financial Services on March 21, 2002. Cleland's testimony exposed many examples of manipulation alleged of Global Crossing and other telecom companies. During his summarized oral remarks, he made three important recommendations to the subcommittee, based upon his firm's research:

> **"Rational Manipulation?" Global Crossing's bankruptcy is a wake up call to Government overseers** of troublesome patterns in the capital markets system for protecting investors and pensioners.
>
> 1. **We must improve our clearly inadequate investment research system; it can't even expose a "trillion dollar fib!"** Investors, who depend on investment research for an objective assessment of the facts and due diligence, were not informed that the single most important trend buttressing Global Crossing's business model and that of all the other data growth stocks was, and had been, hugely overstated and inflated for years! **Gross misrepresentation of demand for data traffic fueled roughly a trillion dollars worth of stock appreciation from 1996 to 2000 that has since cratered.**

---

[53] Ibid., Goto.
[54] Quoted by Wes Vernon, Friday, March 15, 2002. "Congress Finally Ready to Investigate Global Crossing" (NewsMax.com)
[55] Jeff Johnson, Thursday, August 15, 2002. "Union Leaders Accused of Profiting From Insider Trading" (CNSNews.com)
[56] Wednesday, July 24, 2002. "Gov. Gray Davis' Corporate Sleaze" (NewsMax.com)
[57] Ibid., Vernon.

2. The current system also makes it **hard to use investment research that is free of investment banking company bias** that may be better at discovering the problems behind a Global Crossing. ...

3. **We must make our capital markets system much less prone to manipulation**. Growth or "story stocks," like Global Crossing, have become the most prone to manipulation. Moreover, the options-compensation culture we have created for company management can **perversely incent the managements of publicly traded companies to engage in the high-risk behavior** that this hearing is about today.[58]

Along with Mr. Cleland's oral testimony, he submitted for the record a written report that expanded on Precursor's findings. A particular passage described with chilling clarity one of the techniques used to emotionally influence the public stock trader:

The management of growth companies has learned from market experience that their stock price is more dependent on the perception than the reality of future growth. **This means that the price of a growth stock is all about what a company can convince the market that it can do in the future. It is all about "the story."** The best storytellers have the hottest stocks. Or in other words, the tallest tale, that the market can believe wins.[59]

This very "loaded" statement reinforces and confirms some important truths about the stock market and the industry that supports it. First, just as former SEC Chairman Levitt warned in 1998, Cleland found that corporate management uses illusion tactics ("perception") to entice unwary stock traders. Second, because the "story" is what is sold to the public, not the actual value of the company, a means of spreading that story is required, which implicates the company's willing accomplices: the print and broadcast media, brokerages, and market analysts. I say this because it is logical (or naïve) to conclude that, if these purveyors actually *verified* the company's "story" independently *before* touting the stock's merits to the public, perhaps they would not run the "story" at all. In such a case, perhaps, they might actually **dispute** the story. Unfortunately, that's not what happened with Global Crossing, Enron, Priceline, Amazon, and hundreds of other great "story stocks" in the late nineties and on through the technology bubble.

Third, Mr. Cleland's statement confirms that the public stockholder is, at least partially, to blame for not doing the necessary homework on a stock before jumping in. In my experience, acquaintances will believe *the story* from a stranger who has no financial stake in their loss of capital, simply because the stranger has the title "market analyst." Sometimes, it's just *the story* that sells itself. But when confronted with irrefutable facts, mathematics, logic and charts that contradict *the story*, most will buy *the story* anyway, or simply won't want to risk losing a potential fortune. We have already seen the percentage of stock traders that lose money every year. It is obvious that *the story* wins way too often.

Finally, while Cleland does not explicitly state it, I will: many corporate managers (and their accomplices) are in the business of *lying* (telling tall tales) to the public. An occasional emotional appeal based upon a great company story can be tolerated. Lies are another thing entirely. The

---

[58] Scott Cleland, March 21, 2002. Testimony before the House Financial Services Oversight Subcommittee: "Global Crossing's Bankruptcy: A Window Into a Broken System of Protecting Investors," Precursor Group®, Washington D.C., (www.precursorgroup.com). [emphasis his] Quoted with permission of Scott Cleland, founder and CEO of the Precursor Group® and founder and Chairman of the Investorside® Research Association. All rights reserved.
[59] Cleland, p. 8. [emphasis his]

Arthur Anderson accounting scandals have shown us that, in many cases, the alleged lies we were told went far beyond cute stories, but seeped into financial statements as well. Many in the public who actually did their homework on heavily-touted stocks, and accepted in good faith the official financial statements as the truth, were completely duped.

But the testimony continued: Scott Cleland then proceeded to itemize to the House Subcommittee the "tricks of the trade" employed by telecom companies. Get your seatbelt back on before reading this list. But make sure you read each item carefully. These are the weapons aimed at your capital, and whether legal or illegal, **all** are manipulative.

> **There are many stock-enhancing "tricks of the trade" that management can permissibly engage in, sometimes with the help of outside advisors, investment bankers, research analysts, accounting consultants, and lawyers etc., to lift their stock price.** Some of these "tricks of the trade" are:
>
> - Hiding debt off-balance-sheet in special purpose entities (alleged of Enron);
> - Increasing revenue recognition short-term through fiber capacity swaps (alleged of Global Crossing, Enron and others), and equipment/services swaps (alleged of Qwest);
> - Increasing revenue recognition short-term with 200% equipment vendor-financing (alleged of many equipment companies);
> - Writing off costs to improve forward-looking results (alleged of WorldCom and many others);
> - Writing off over $50 billion in goodwill and saying it doesn't matter (alleged of JDS Uniphase);
> - Continuing to book revenues from former customers (alleged of Winstar);
> - Backdating revenues to maintain the expected revenue growth trajectory (alleged of MicroStrategy);
> - Creating tracking stocks to supposedly 'unlock shareholder value' (WorldCom and Sprint);
> - Buying a company solely to acquire revenues to avoid a debt triggering covenant (alleged of Level 3);
> - Selling an asset to avoid a debt triggering covenant (alleged of Sprint);
> - Managing earnings estimates (alleged of Cisco and many others);
> - Allowing supportive analysts to see more financial detail than non-supportive analysts (alleged of WorldCom);
> - Promoting pro-forma financial performance rather than actual GAAP results (alleged of many companies);
> - Declaring that the company has "no visibility" about future demand while simultaneously expressing confidence about eventually returning to 30% plus growth (alleged of Cisco);
> - And the list can go on and on.[60]

The evidence of market manipulation presented so far is not exhaustive - literally hundreds of companies are routinely manipulated by others, or are party to manipulation. Thousands of innocent companies are hurt by the market's reaction to the manipulations of a few. Millions of public stock traders lose their total investments, whether they trade in individual stocks or through mutual funds. At the *macro* and *micro* levels, much of the manipulation we have seen is

---

[60] Cleland, p. 9. [emphasis his] (the abbreviation, GAAP, stands for "generally accepted accounting principles.")

performed out of the control of the public. In other words, the actions of some public corporations and their supporting cast members in the brokerages and media outlets are designed for "mass consumption," hurting entire industries and every shareholder attached to them.

But manipulation can also occur at the *sub-micro* level, between you and your stockbroker. While it is true that many brokers and analysts and, yes, even some media personalities, are honest and wish the best of success for their customers, many scams have been, and are, perpetrated on the unwary. Each level within the investment industry is motivated by different factors, resulting in a "domino effect," with you - the individual stockholder - acting as the last domino in the chain.

The Domino Effect

Brokers are motivated to make commissions - some are forced to make daily quotas in order to keep their jobs - compelling them to tout the day's "hot stocks" to traders. Market analysts are motivated to keep their clients, for whom they calculate ratings and earnings estimates; plus, many analysts wish to remain "newsworthy" to market journals and TV shows in order to be labeled as experts. The media, of course, is motivated by ratings, which is easily enhanced by always having "hot stocks" to track and government reports to blame for movements in the overall market. Corporate insiders are motivated by the need to maximize earnings (or the appearance thereof) in order to enhance stockholder value, or their own stock option values. Mutual fund managers and other institutional portfolio managers are motivated to buy at the bottom and sell at the top, before the public gets wind of their intent; thus they buy "quietly" in small amounts over long periods of time, but sell quickly in large blocks. The domino effect of incentives to over-hype stocks is systemic, and dangerous to those in the public who rely on so-called "experts" for their trading decisions.

Dr. Martin Weiss compiled a list of techniques and scams the industry uses to mislead investors. The underlying motivations for these techniques are clear. With his publisher's permission, I have summarized his findings below:[61]

- **Goodwill Distortion** - When one company buys another company, the accountants allocate the purchase price on the buying company's balance sheet as "goodwill," which they treat as an "asset" right along side "cash" and other tangibles. However, "goodwill" has no substance. It is a "fiction" of accounting. Instead of amortizing their purchase over ten years, they are often tempted to stretch it to 40 years (the legal limit), reducing the drag on net income. This act exaggerates earnings and potentially deceives the vast majority of the stock-buying public, who may not understand how to read corporate balance sheets.

- **Pooling of Interest** - Instead of creating goodwill accounts, many companies just "pool their interests" by combining their assets into one big account, burying the huge overstatement of values in their balance sheets. This leaves shareholders believing that a company is worth far more than it is, with no clear way to discover the truth. Plus, without a goodwill account to charge against earnings, the company is free to exaggerate earnings further. Alleged uses of this gimmick were seen recently with Yahoo! buying Geocities, Lucent Technologies buying Ascend Communications, Cisco Systems buying Cerent, and many others.

- **Padded Sales Reports** - Company A offers to "sell" some equipment to Company B for, say, $2 million. To sweeten the deal, Company A offers to install the equipment

---

[61] Weiss, pp. 6-20.

for free, train the users for free, and compensate Company B with a check for $100,000 to cover their "ancillary" expenses. Oh yes, instead of Company B - a small firm - having to actually *pay* the $2 million, all it has to do is give Company A five-percent of its stock. Company A - a Fortune 500 firm - now gets to "book" $2 million in sales it will never be paid for, boosting its reported sales for the upcoming quarterly "confession" season. This is just one method used to lure investors who live and die by a company's "fundamentals."

- **Options Boondoggles** - Today's corporate officers, as we have seen, are often compensated with stock options as incentives to guide the company toward success, or the appearance of success. As long as the stock price is rising, everything is OK. But what if the price is falling? Boards practice what is called "rolling down the strike price" which replaces an officer's options to buy at $20 (the strike price) with options to buy at $5 or $10, letting the officer off the hook. For officers, this is a "no lose" situation. For shareholders, it's "no win."

- **"Purchased" Stock Ratings** - The common scenario today is to distort a corporation's books as much as possible, hiding the negatives, and then to "...add on a whole new layer of hype and distortion."[62] A whole new breed of investment bankers and underwriters now act as promoters rather than independent handlers of new stock issues and IPOs. Rather than earning commissions on the volume of shares placed, these firms now earn a percentage of the total take, giving them a vested interest in touting and hyping the stock. Instead of being objective, they now "upgrade" and "downgrade" a stock to the public in a manner that best makes money for their clients, and themselves. The analysts working for these firms are, thus, motivated to deceive and are penalized for their honesty. According to the *Wall Street Journal*, for example, Morgan Stanley received bigger bonuses when they made "a positive contribution to underwriting revenues." Similarly, Morgan Stanley held back promotions, or actually demoted analysts who refused to suppress negative information about stocks the firm was handling.[63] During the "technology bubble" in 2000 and 2001, for example, one analyst at Goldman Sachs issued 11 "gloriously positive" ratings on stocks that ended up losing 75 percent of their value. In fact, the analyst's best performer lost 71 percent, his worst, 99.8 percent. Oh yes, the analyst was paid $20 million for his efforts.

- **Broker Swindles** - In 1994, the General Accounting Office (GAO) conducted an intensive study of the nation's stockbrokers. They found that almost 10,000 active brokers had been caught swindling their clients - and that's just the ones the GAO caught.[64] Methods used include "churning," making unauthorized trades, overstating the value of accounts between statements, faking statements, collecting funds for trades then using the money for personal or unauthorized purposes, forgery, and others. The GAO study warned that only 1 in 10 such crimes committed by brokers are ever detected, reported or prosecuted.

- **Ignored Warnings** - Brokers are warned of impending problems with a stock, but do not pass the information on to their clients until they have completed a campaign of hyping the stock so they - the brokers - can liquidate their holdings in that stock. TV market commentators keep their ratings up by concentrating on "good news" and not on negative earnings warnings. Often, visiting analysts on their shows will brush aside negative news with "plausible" explanations (true or not), temporarily postponing the day of reckoning for a stock - until it is too late.

---

[62] Gretchen Morgenson, December 31, 2000. "How Did So Many Get It So Wrong?" (New York Times).

[63] Michael Siconolfi, July 14, 1992. "Under Pressure: at Morgan Stanley, Analysts Were Urged to Soften Harsh Views" (Wall Street Journal), p. A1.

[64] U.S. Government Accounting Office, "Securities Markets: Actions Needed to Better Protect Investors against Unscrupulous Brokers" (GAO/GGD-94-208 - www.gao.gov)

Although the above techniques paint a very pessimistic view of investment professionals, I have already stated that many of these professionals are honest and have your best interests at heart. The question is: *which ones*? Even if we, as public investors, are aware of these schemes, we are left with the dilemma of trying to read the motives of the professionals who make their living advising us. In my opinion, only a *Mercenary* attitude can protect you in this environment: **do your own research and trust no advice but your own.**

But, do you trust yourself? Unfortunately, the most dangerous threat to our capital often lurks so close to us that, if we didn't duck our heads now and then, we'd be hit by an enemy we see in the mirror every morning.

Mental Tricks

We have discussed the motivations of corporation officers, brokers, fund managers, the media, market analysts, and others in the profession who often have a conflict of interest with their shareholders. While it is easy to understand their motivations, originating from the same greed and fear that we feel, we must learn to defend against them. To do this, we must understand our own motivations to buy or sell a stock; or rather, we must discover how our motivation is influenced.

The Power of Mob Psychology

It all comes down to marketing, which is more a study of the human mind than a means of selling goods and services. For example, we already know that marketing techniques can affect us, causing us to want things, or to want one brand over another, or to want something now rather than later. The same techniques can be used to induce us to buy or sell stocks at the wrong time, benefiting only the marketers or their clients. These are all weapons that the alert *Stock Market Mercenary* must evade.

One successful investor made a lifetime study of the effects of mob psychology on the individual investor, and developed a unique *Contrarian* strategy to counter them. When Ted Warren began to invest in stocks in the 1930s, he had a sixth-grade education, was a common laborer, and had just a few hundred dollars to his name. His study of human reactions to the machinations of market professionals began with his *own* reactions, and his subsequent desires to buy or sell at the wrong times. By the mid-1960s, Warren was a multi-millionaire, and began writing a manuscript of his findings and resulting strategies, published many years later by The Ted Warren Corporation and titled *How To Make the Stock Market Make Money for You.*[65] This book is *must reading* for *Stock Market Mercenaries*.

According to Ted Warren, most stockholders do what comes "naturally." Unfortunately, history shows us that, what is "natural" psychologically, is often wrong financially. Over the years, Warren correlated the natural responses to the most common situations encountered by stock traders. I have consolidated and summarized these situations and the relevant responses in the figure below. I believe that many of these situations and responses will seem familiar to you.

---

[65] Ted Warren, 1966. "How To Make the Stock Market Make Money For You" (The Ted Warren Corporation, Grants Pass, OR, 541-955-2779, 3rd edition, 1998).

Situation	Natural Response
Sees a stock is at the bottom for a long time.	Questions the reason; is suspicious of unseen facts; passes up a bargain.
Owns a stock that is at the bottom for a long time.	Gets discouraged; sells at, or below break-even.
Owns a stock that has been at the bottom but now begins to rise.	Feels "lucky" and sells at a small profit; or continues to hold amidst "positive" reports; allows himself to "fall in love" with the stock; starts feeling confident of his picking ability.
Owns a stock that is at the top, but hasn't sold it, and now it is declining.	Thinks the price will come back up; sets sell price too high.
Sold the stock at or near the top ("lucky").	Compelled to buy it back too soon, because it appears low compared to the recent high.
Sees a stock he thinks will rise quickly (due to media hype, etc.)	Waits for some upside movement to "prove" he's right; buys too late; takes a loss.
Sees a stock with recent, fast movement and heavy trading volume.	The majority must be right; buys the stock, again, too late. (Mob psychology wins)
Bought a stock too late.	Slow to decide because he was so positive he was right; loss increases over time.
Sells a stock soon after buying it too late.	If stock rallies after he sold, thinks it was a mistake to have sold; if stock drops after he sold, knows it was a mistake to have bought in the first place.
Holds a stock that's dropping far below purchase price.	Develops hatred for the "offending" stock and sells at a severe loss.
Owns many stocks during a market panic.	Thinks the market cannot go up; sells at a loss. (Mob psychology wins)
Missed opportunity to sell a stock at a fair price.	Sells when it again reaches that price, even though it is the wrong place to sell.
Is considering a stock to buy.	Thinks "fundamentals" are key to decision, since that's what the experts say. (Mob psychology wins) Ignores long-term charts that show where a stock has been and where it is capable of going; Asks broker to suggest a good stock; looks for hot tips, rumors, headlines, and TV analysts.

FIGURE 3-9. Summary of Ted Warren's "Natural Responses" to Stock Trading Situations.[66]

Did you notice the common thread in the "natural" responses to these situations? In every case, our human psychology allows *emotions* to dictate the next move, right or wrong. What are those emotions? Greed and fear. To defend against our natural instincts, Ted Warren advocated the use of long-term charts to either prove or disprove the validity of a trading decision. Since we have shown that a company's fundamentals (financial statements, company "story," financial

---

[66] Warren, pp. 3-4.

ratios, etc.) are subject to manipulation and deceit, few indicators remain that better illustrate the potential of a stock than its long-term price chart.

Unfortunately, most stockbrokers and analysts will tell you that reading a stock chart is fruitless effort, that you cannot expect a chart of "past activity" to indicate anything the stock can do in the future. As you will see later, not only are charts considered a waste of time by investment professionals, but the advocacy of using charts in the formulation of trading strategies is a violation of SEC regulations! This, in my opinion, is the **only** reason why Ted Warren's investment philosophy is not required reading in every university and business school.

On TV stock market shows, the charts used to illustrate the price movements of a stock are usually one, three or six-month views - extremely short-term samples. Rarely do you get to see the entire history of a stock. But Ted Warren's "chartist" philosophy can be summarized in one quote by Sir Winston Churchill: "The farther backward you can look, the farther forward you can see."[67]

Remember your mother telling you not to pick up that piece of candy on the floor because, "you don't know where it's been?" Well, listen to your mother. **Knowing where a stock has been offers proof of what is possible, even if it doesn't guarantee a future outcome.** Further, since we have shown clear evidence of price manipulation by insiders and institutions, it is likely that such manipulation will appear on a company's long-term stock chart. *Stock Market Mercenaries* use any weapon available to uncover such manipulation and, if possible, to profit from it.

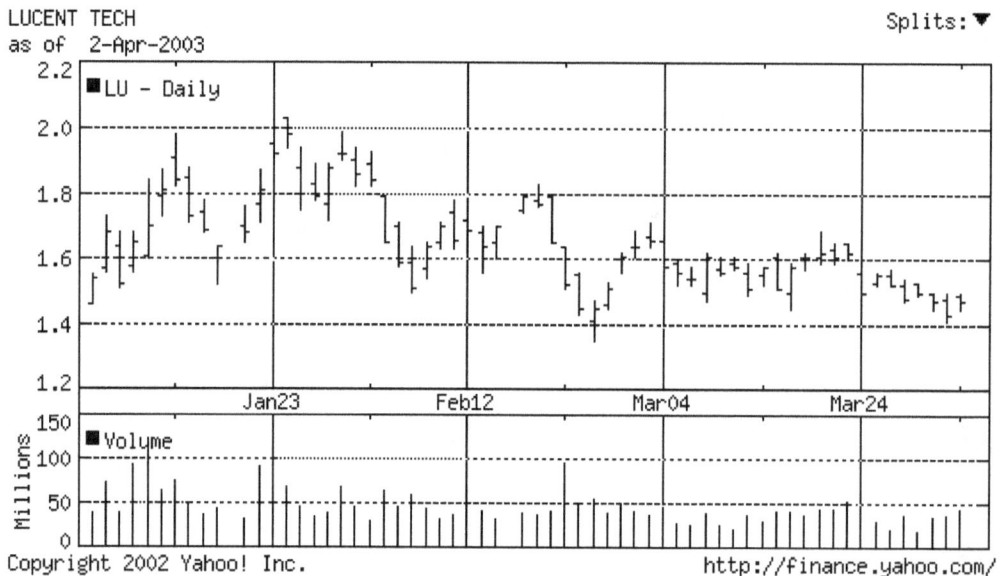

FIGURE 3-10. 3-month split-adjusted price history of Lucent Technologies (LU) as of April 2, 2003. [Reproduced with permission of Yahoo! Inc. © 2003 by Yahoo! Inc. YAHOO! and the YAHOO! logo are trademarks of Yahoo! Inc.]

How misleading can short-term charts be? Take the rather "pessimistic" three-month chart of Lucent Technologies, for example (Figure 3-10). If your price history research is limited to this view, you would naturally conclude that the stock is currently on a downtrend. You might also conclude that this stock trades in a range from just under $1.40 to just over $2.00. If you already

---

[67] Winston Churchill, quoted by James C. Humes, 1982. "Churchill: Speaker of the Century" (Scarborough Books, New York, NY)

owned this stock, having purchased it near the $2.00 mark, how would you feel right now about your investment? In other words, what would be your "natural response?"

If you were an institutional investor, hoping to accumulate more shares of Lucent at cheap prices, would this chart be a good one to show the public? The fact is that TV market shows use short-term charts like this one all the time, telling only *part* of the story. In this case, the "part" of the story being told would likely have a "discouraging" effect on the public's psychology.

But wait! What if your view of Lucent Technologies spanned the past *six months*, as seen in Figure 3-11? Based on this chart, would you still feel discouraged? Since it is obvious that this stock has been much lower than the current $1.50 price, you might conclude that you are near the top. Or, had you purchased this stock near the $2.00 mark, you might feel that you missed your opportunity to make a profit, and are now contemplating selling it at a loss. If you had bought it near $1.00, however, you would be ecstatic to be sitting at a 50-percent profit right now. But, are any of these responses valid?

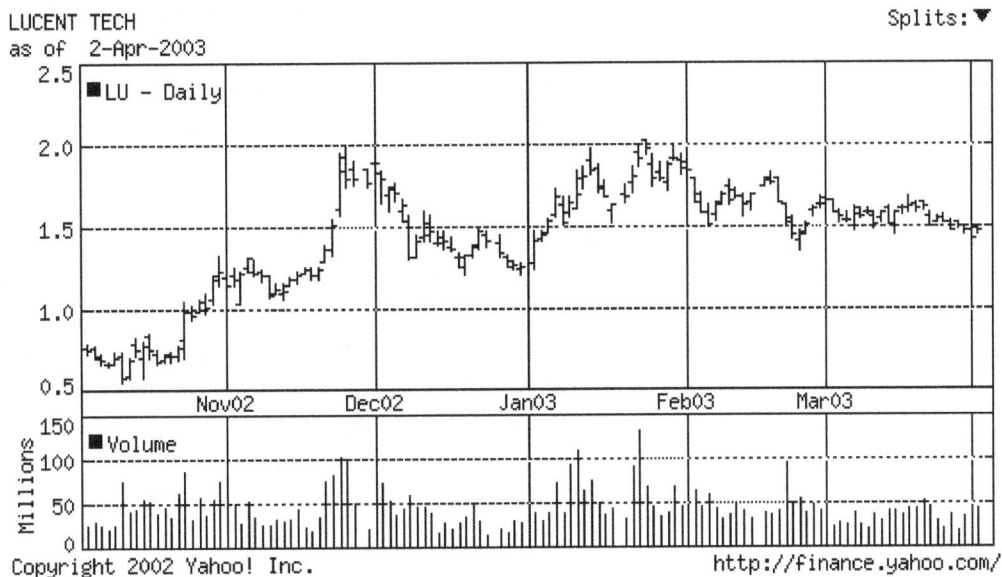

FIGURE 3-11. 6-month split-adjusted price history of Lucent Technologies (LU) as of April 2, 2003. [Reproduced with permission of Yahoo! Inc. © 2003 by Yahoo! Inc. YAHOO! and the YAHOO! logo are trademarks of Yahoo! Inc.]

It is amazing what six more months can do to one's perspective! Check out Lucent's *one-year* chart below (Figure 3-12). While the six-month chart indicated that the current price was within 50-cents of the top, the one-year view shows that Lucent is much nearer the bottom and that the "top" is really above $4.00. While this view is definitely more revealing than the previous short-term charts, it still does not tell the whole story. Yet this is the typical view published in most market journals and displayed on TV shows as a "long-term" history, and is the common view promoted by market analysts.

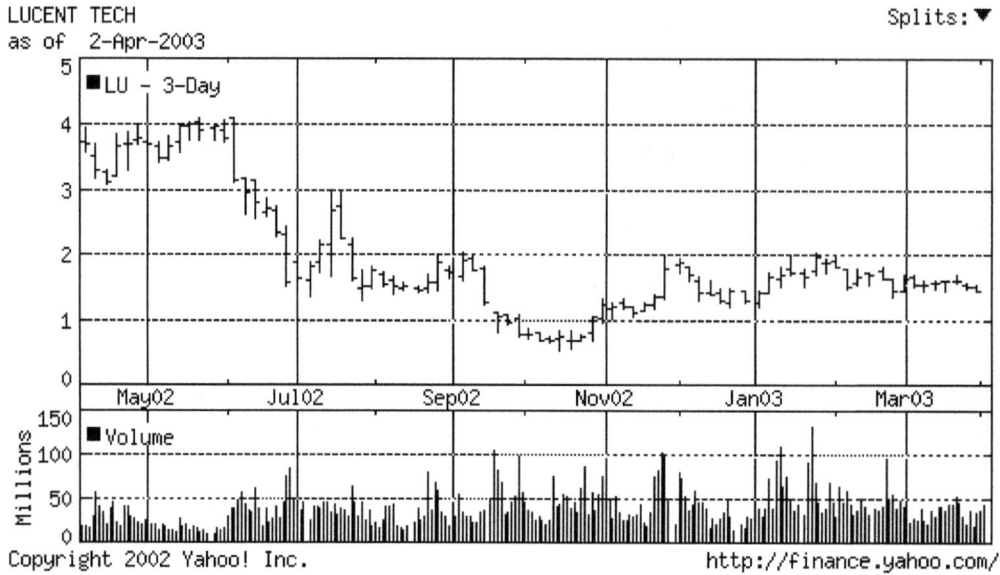

FIGURE 3-12. 1-year split-adjusted price history of Lucent Technologies (LU) as of April 2, 2003. [Reproduced with permission of Yahoo! Inc. © 2003 by Yahoo! Inc. YAHOO! and the YAHOO! logo are trademarks of Yahoo! Inc.]

In keeping with Churchill's philosophy, that is, looking as far into the past as possible to determine potential for the future, I have included a total-history chart of Lucent in Figure 3-13. Note that today's price of $1.50 is a far cry from the 60-plus dollar top Lucent enjoyed just before the Tech-Bubble burst in early-2000. Looking at the "big picture," this stock is near the historical bottom. Thus, if your goal as a *Stock Market Mercenary* is to "buy low and sell high," what would be your motivation right now with Lucent stock? More importantly, if you were motivated to buy this stock, would the objective long-term chart data below validate that decision more accurately than the three, six, or twelve-month charts we've seen?

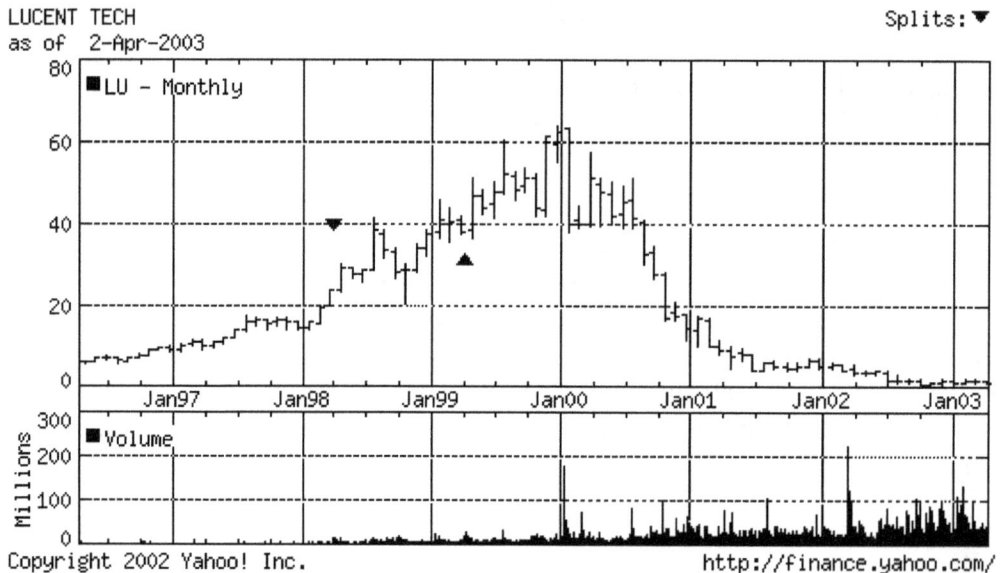

FIGURE 3-13. Total split-adjusted price history of Lucent Technologies (LU) as of April 2, 2003. [Reproduced with permission of Yahoo! Inc. © 2003 by Yahoo! Inc. YAHOO! and the YAHOO! logo are trademarks of Yahoo! Inc.]

Ted Warren's success at being a *Contrarian* stemmed from anticipating the mob psychology and doing the opposite, which required strict emotional discipline. For example, as I write this section, the headlines and TV analysts are playing down the value of Lucent stock. It's at or near recent lows, after all, and it wouldn't be there if the company was doing well. That's the "logic" I'm hearing, anyway. The chart shown today on TV was a three-month view, which definitely supported the premise that the stock was trending downward. If you currently owned this stock, the "message" from these investment professionals was to sell it and take your losses. If you were contemplating buying this stock, the message was to look elsewhere because the company is "unloved" right now.

Meanwhile, *Mercenaries* would be tracking this stock closely, knowing that it was approaching **the perfect place to buy: near its historical bottom, where nobody but the insiders and institutions want it, at a time when the company is in disrepute**. We will discuss this concept further in the next two chapters.

It should now be clear that investment professionals know all about "mob psychology." They know what marketing buttons to push to affect the public's emotions. They know the difference between a short-term and a long-term chart. They know how to tout a losing stock. And, *some of these professionals actually believe that the public is stupid*. They must, or we wouldn't have clear examples like *Ecogen*.

The Ecogen Manipulation

During the period we identified as the "technology bubble," biotechnology firms followed the same basic patterns as did the dot-coms. Many bio-techs came and went as they enticed traders with wild new medical or chemical breakthroughs, only to disappoint later with failed clinical trials or denied F.D.A. approvals. One such company was *Ecogen, Inc.*, (stock symbol EECN) which manufactured "environmentally compatible" pest-control products. Matt Morsa, editor of a newsletter called *The Investolator*®, published by The Ted Warren Corporation, and based on Warren's method, chronicled the Ecogen manipulation:[68]

On January 5, 2000, the *PRNewswire* broadcast the headline, "Ecogen Confirms Monsanto Is Using its BT Toxin Gene." Before the headline came out, Ecogen was selling for $1.25. By the end of the day, the stock had doubled to $2.50, fading back over the next few weeks to under $2. Later, Ecogen got caught up in the technology feeding frenzy and, by March 17th, was starting down from its high of $5.875, continuing its slide to hit a new bottom in June, below a dollar, where it proceeded sideways all summer.

On July 10th, a headline appeared stating, "Philippe Katz, Director buys 7,500 shares between June 21-22." Mind you, the stock was selling below a dollar, so such a small insider purchase was negligible and wouldn't have affected the price. But, it was the *psychological* effect the insiders were looking for - worth a low-risk sucker play. If the price went up in the future as a result of some positive story, these 7,500 shares along with thousands of others held by insiders could be dumped.

Sure enough, on August 31, 2000, a story broke with the headline, "Ecogen Confirms Monsanto Is Using its BT Toxin Gene." **The same story, word-for-word, that had been used**

---

[68] Matt Morsa, October 2000. "A Classic Case of Manipulation" (The Investolator®, Grants Pass, OR)

eight months earlier was now being used again to trick the public. It worked. The morning this headline broke, the stock immediately shot up to $2.50, and the insiders dumped their shares at 150 percent profit. But that's not all!

A few days later, on September 11th, another story reported that Ecogen was being de-listed to the "penny stock" market (OTC Bulletin Board) for not meeting NASDAQ's minimum price requirements. Based on that story, the price dropped immediately to 56-cents. Once again, the public had been fleeced. Two and a half years later, as of this writing, Ecogen is operating under stock symbol ECGN and is selling for 11 cents.

There are hundreds of examples of these "mental tricks" played on public stock traders every year, with the full support of brokers, analysts, and the media. The public loses billions of dollars every year as a result.

Summary

If you have survived your training thus far, then you know that stock market manipulation does occur, with regularity, that it has its roots in the very foundations of our capitalistic system, that no amount of regulation can stop it, and that most members of the public are victimized by it. You also know that insiders and institutional investors have the means, the motive, and the opportunity to affect the prices of stocks, while stockbrokers and analysts are motivated to help them get away with it. Further, you know that you cannot trust the stock market hype you are fed by the media, nor most published corporate earnings reports, nor recommendations given by stockbrokers and market analysts. Finally, you know that your own psychology, and your emotions, are routinely used against you, causing you to make the wrong trading decisions.

The next step in your *Mercenary* training is to analyze and compare the most popular investment strategies available, and to learn which of these strategies the industry - and the federal government - doesn't want you to use.

Chapter 4: The Popular Strategies

Finding winning methods, despite an industry bent on hiding them.

In the previous chapters, I exposed some of the "bad news" of stock investing against which every *Stock Market Mercenary* should be prepared. By now you should know that, to survive in this environment, you must earn sufficient profits to overcome rampant market manipulation, taxes and inflation that drain your wealth. You have also seen that, due to widespread unethical accounting practices, it can be hazardous to your portfolio to rely on the integrity of corporate financial statements. Finally, you have seen the results of investing in a stock solely based upon the company's story, compelling as it may be.

Your remaining task, then, is to find investment strategies that are 1) profitable, 2) logical and objective, 3) low-risk, and 4) easy to understand. According to Michael Sincere, in *101 Investment Lessons From the Wizards of Wall Street*, to succeed, you must choose a strategy based on solid results, create a written set of rules to prevent emotions from clouding your judgment, and then stick with your strategy no matter what. Mr. Sincere says that the secret to successful investing can be summarized in one word: Discipline.[70]

Most investment strategies are based upon one or more of the methods discussed in this chapter. Some are very "technical" in nature, requiring little if any personal judgment, while others require a high degree of subjective reasoning to make the final stock picks. Still others are so complicated that you almost need degrees in mathematics, accounting, economics and computer science to uncover the right investments.

Before we analyze the most popular strategies, there are a few *universal rules* that I urge you to consider as part of any investment strategy you develop. Many of these principles of sound investing derive from *common sense*, not from a particular method or philosophy. You will see again that I have included some of the wit and wisdom of Warren Buffett in this chapter. In Chapter 1, I described the "homework" all stock traders should do - in short: *find those who succeed in the market, learn how they do it, and then ride their coattails.* Despite any differences of opinion I may have with Mr. Buffett's investment philosophy, it is hard to ignore his success as an investor, thus, I have read everything I could find about the man and his methods, including his annual reports and letters to Berkshire Hathaway's shareholders. It is natural, therefore, that some of his wisdom has "absorbed" over the years.

---

[69] Warren Buffett, quoted by Linda Grant, "The $4 Billion Regular Guy," The Los Angeles Times Magazine, April 7, 1991, p. 58.

[70] Michael Sincere, 1999. "101 Investment Lessons From the Wizards of Wall Street" (The Career Press, Inc., Franklin Lakes, NJ), pp. 15-25. Used with permission of the publisher. © 1999 Michael Sincere. All rights reserved.

Universal Rules of Sound Investing

Some of the best investment theories ever devised, according to Warren Buffett, were written by Benjamin Graham, but they are seldom taught in college curriculums today because,

> ...It's not difficult enough. So, instead, something is taught that is difficult but not useful. The business schools reward complex behavior more than simple behavior, but simple behavior is more effective.[71]

Buffett's company, Berkshire Hathaway, has a reputation for buying out companies more often than simply investing in them (Geico Insurance, See's Candies, Dairy Queen, and many others are Berkshire companies). When making such purchases, the negotiations are done quietly, and are usually consummated for no more than ten times annual earnings (an equivalent to a 10 P/E ratio). For example, when Berkshire acquired Central States Indemnity Co. in 1992, its CEO, William Kizer, described the negotiations this way:

> The price he quoted us was that he buys companies for 10 times earnings. I suggested, "Well, last year we made $10 million, so if my multiplication is right, that's $100 million," and I gulped. And he said "Okay." And I said "$125 million?" He said, "You're too late."[72]

Next, we should always buy when the public is headed the other way. In other words, Buffett believes we should take advantage of *Contrarian* opportunities:

> Most people get interested in stocks when everyone else is. The time to get interested is when no one else is. You can't buy what is popular and do well.[73]

Further, Buffett rarely buys a company, nor any shares of a company, that he doesn't clearly comprehend. If the business model cannot be explained to a non-professional on a cocktail napkin over lunch, then it's too complicated to own (Enron and Global Crossing are recent examples of companies that nobody - not even the corporate officers - could easily explain). On this topic, in his understated style, Buffett said, "I want to be able to explain my mistakes. This means I do only the things I completely understand."[74]

The following rules are not necessarily derived from Mr. Buffett's philosophy, but are shared by many successful investors.

You must understand and accept the risks of owning stocks. Most strategies are designed to manage risk, or to minimize it, but no strategy can eliminate risk. Bodybuilders teach us that, to build muscles we must first inflict stress and pain on them. Likewise, successful stock investing requires that we endure the risk (and associated stress) of potentially losing our capital (pain) in order to reap future rewards. This *universal rule*, then, asks you to take a calculated risk with money you can cheerfully lose. In fact, if your capital cannot be "cheerfully" lost, then you should not be risking it.

One way to minimize risks is to diversify your portfolio. Investing all your capital in one or two stocks can be dangerous. Smart investors spread their risk among 10 or 12 different stocks,

---

[71] Warren Buffet speech, December 6, 1994, New York Society of Security Analysts.

[72] Jim Rasmussen, October 21, 1992. "Hometown Deal Pleases Buffett" (Omaha World-Herald), p. 16.

[73] Warren Buffett, quoted by Ann Hughey, April 1, 1985. "Omaha's Plain Dealer" (Newsweek), p. 56.

[74] Warren Buffett, quoted by Robert Dorr, December 5, 1968. "Buffett Quickly Unloaded First Three Stock Shares" (Omaha World-Herald)

or even more, at a time. Even smarter investors make sure they own no more than two stocks from the same industry or business sector. For example, they might only hold one telecom stock, two food producers, one energy company, and so on. Lowering risk may be the primary reason to diversify, but there is another important benefit: the more market segments you hold stock in, the better your chances of owning a winning stock. Why? After a major earthquake, for example, insurance stocks may tumble while construction services may skyrocket. There always seems to be one industry doing well while others are suffering. Another way to diversify is to invest in stock index funds, which often represent hundreds of stocks from many industries.

Finally, it makes a lot of sense to invest in companies that actually create new and tangible wealth. With a trend in the United States toward service industries, as opposed to the manufacturing sector, most companies appear to just do each other's laundry. They transfer wealth around, but don't actually produce anything new. For example, industries that produce new wealth include *mining, drilling, agriculture* (along with ranching and fishing), *manufacturing* and *construction*. Some find and extract raw materials from the Earth; others breed and feed animals; and still others take raw materials and produce something more valuable than the sum of its parts. You could probably add alternative energy producers to the list, since they "harvest" wind, water or solar energy in its natural state and convert it to a salable commodity. Next, you could add companies that directly supply or support those industries producing the new wealth, including software development firms that "mine" intellectual property to produce useful tools.

As each headline of a corporate failure or fraud has appeared in the media, I have found myself asking: "Did this company actually create new wealth?" Not surprisingly, the answer is "no" most of the time. For example, what new wealth did Enron, Global Crossing and Priceline.com actually produce? One sold someone else's (or non-existent) energy; one sold the use of undersea network cables (can you say "rented electrons?"), and one sold empty seats on airplanes. Each did someone else's laundry. Meanwhile, the companies doing the best since spring of 2000 were traditional brick-and-mortar manufacturers, oil and mining firms, homebuilders, textiles, and food producers. The bottom line to this rule is: wealth **producers** survive in bad economies better than wealth **passers**.

There are exceptions to every rule, of course, and (confession is good for the soul) I have broken this rule a time or two. Real wealth producers can be mismanaged as badly as any other company, and some service industries - especially those with strong sales forces - can outperform brick-and-mortar businesses. So, although I don't always heed my own advice on this rule, in general terms and in historical context, it is a sound universal principle.

Summarizing the universal rules of sound investing, *Stock Market Mercenaries* will:

- **Stick to simple methods;**

- **Buy at 10-times annual earnings (10 P/E) or lower;**

- **Buy when everyone else is selling; sell when everyone else is buying;**

- **Buy only companies whose business model they understand;**

- **Be willing to cheerfully take a calculated risk;**

- **Diversify holdings with stocks from many different market segments;**

- **Buy companies that produce real wealth, or that directly support such companies.**

While these rules will help you reduce your risk of loss, they will not pinpoint a precise collection of stocks worthy of your capital, nor will they help you properly time your trades. Those functions demand more specific strategies. I will briefly cover the most popular of these strategies and expose some "fatal flaws" that often turn public investors into victims.

Value Investing

Benjamin Graham is widely considered the "grandfather" of value investing. He consistently searched for stocks selling at prices significantly below the companies' worth, and invested in such a way as to protect his original capital while taking advantage of long-term profits. Some believe that John Burr Williams actually codified the "intrinsic value method," which Graham later popularized in his books and classrooms at Columbia University. But, until I began my equities research, I had never heard of Mr. Williams.

The value investor finds the best bargains in a slow, flat market. Thus, at times, value investing can generate rather *Contrarian* stock picks. The key ingredient to this strategy is the "fair value" of the company, which requires the evaluation of both objective and subjective measurements. Low P/E ratios and high dividend yields are two - of many - objective factors. Others include low price-to-book (PTB) and high book-to-market (BTM) ratios, which are simply the inverse of each other (PTB = stock price ÷ book value per share; BTM = book value per share ÷ stock price). Another key calculation is the ten-year discounted cash flow analysis, which (of course) assumes you can find the past ten years' worth of financials on the company.

Some value fund managers - encouraged by recent statistical studies - believe that a small company with a high BTM ratio has a higher potential return than any large company with the same (or better) BTM, subject to all the other "fair value" calculations.

Value investors believe that the difference between the value of a stock and its price is the "margin of safety." Patience is also key to this strategy, as value investors will hold an out-of-favor or depressed stock for years until it reaches a level they calculate is the "fair value." The end result of a "value" stock analysis is a set of price ranges at which one would buy, hold, or sell the stock. Based upon your calculations, you would conclude that any stock price well-below fair value indicated a buy; a price slightly below to slightly above fair value would indicate a hold; and any price significantly above fair value would indicate a sell. Reaching these conclusions, however, is not a trivial pursuit. Imagine multiplying this effort across the 5,000 top stocks listed on the major exchanges!

Subjectively, value investors believe that they must understand both the underlying business and all the competition within the company's business sector, since their philosophy includes the premise that they must act as if they were buying the entire company, not just a few of its shares.[75]

Warren Buffett is one of the most famous advocates of Graham's theories. As Berkshire Hathaway has grown, however, Buffett has been forced to "scale" the philosophy to meet his needs, thus diverging a little from some of Graham's principles. So, what works for Buffett may or may not work for the average public stock trader. One of Buffett's key differences is his preference for "simple behaviors" in stock picking. In 1997, Buffett described how simple (in principle anyway) successful investing can be:

---

[75] Sincere, p. 16.

> The art of investing in public companies successfully is little different from the art of successfully acquiring subsidiaries. In each case you simply want to acquire, at a sensible price, a business with excellent economics and able, honest management. Thereafter, you need only monitor whether these qualities are being preserved.[76]

Note the "simple" requirement to determine a "sensible price," calculate whether a company has "excellent economics," and discover whether the company's management is able and honest! Of all the stock investment strategies I have studied, few can be more complicated than value investing! One value fund manager advocates the use of nearly 250 different data points, resulting in over twenty ratios and indicators, to formulate his "fair value" price ranges.

On calculating a company's "intrinsic value," even Buffett believes that it's easier said than done:

> Intrinsic value can be defined simply: It is the discounted value of the cash that can be taken out of a business during its remaining life. The calculation of intrinsic value, though, is not so simple. As our definition suggests, intrinsic value is an estimate rather than a precise figure, and it is additionally an estimate that must be changed if interest rates move or forecasts of future cash flows are revised. Two people looking at the same set of facts, moreover ... will almost inevitably come up with at least slightly different intrinsic value figures.[77]

Buffett also believes that reliance on the book value of a company is "meaningless as an indicator of intrinsic value."[78] Thus, even among professional users of value investing, there are differences of opinion. While debate is a good thing, of course, the public is left confused over which "guru" to believe. And a confused public will misuse the method, or abandon it completely.

Although Berkshire Hathaway does hold minority positions in a few companies (e.g., Coca Cola, American Express), Buffett's primary goal is to purchase entire companies with management teams intact, thus he is able to gain access to corporate information on buyout candidates that may or may not be available to the individual investor at the time of acquisition.

The biggest downside to value investing, of course, is that one must rely on a company's balance sheets, income statements, and cash flow statements to complete the fair value calculations. As we have illustrated, these statements can be misleading, manipulated, or outright falsehoods in at least 31 percent of the *known* cases. Most company information considered suitable for the public is released too late for intelligent action, or is too "optimistic" to be believed.

One thing is certain: **none** of the top value fund managers has consistently beat the returns from index funds every year, and very few value fund managers have made a profit every year. Why? Because neither the stock market nor fund managers are "efficient!" For example, index funds (which track the broader market) tend to outperform mutual funds during bull markets. During bear markets, many indexes still outperform managed funds, but since managers can

---

[76] Warren Buffett, February 28, 1997. "Berkshire Hathaway Inc - Chairman's Letter - 1996" (www.berkshirehathaway.com/letters/1996.html) Used by permission.
[77] Warren Buffett, June, 1996. "Berkshire Hathaway Inc - An Owner's Manual" (www.berkshirehathaway.com/1996ar/manual.html) Used by permission.
[78] Ibid.

"cherry-pick" stocks (unlike indexes), there are opportunities to profit during general downtrends.

Despite all its negatives, value investing is the strategy most quoted by brokers, analysts, TV commentators, and other professionals who are paid to influence the trading public. However, since the public makes the wrong trading decisions over 90 percent of the time, one must ask whether the advice itself is flawed, or is too complicated, or whether the public bothers to follow it. **It is interesting to note that the strongest advocates of value investing are those who do it full-time.** Based upon the sheer volume of data required to accurately estimate the value of each prospective company and the research needed to evaluate the quality of the company's management team, an individual with a job and a family will be hard-pressed to find the time necessary to be successful at this strategy.

Perhaps this is why, in his "Chairman's Letter" to Berkshire Hathaway shareholders in February, 1997, Warren Buffett gave some advice to those contemplating investing on their own:

> Most investors, both institutional and individual, will find that the best way to own common stocks is through an index fund that charges minimal fees. Those following this path are sure to beat the net results (after fees and expenses) delivered by the great majority of investment professionals.[79]

Growth Investing

To qualify as a "growth" company, it must already be growing and is expected to grow even faster in the future. Any company of any size, within any industry, can qualify as long as it has above-average sales, earnings, or market share. The best companies for this strategy are growing by at least 15 percent per year and are expected to continue at that pace. It doesn't matter if a stock has a high P/E ratio as long as the company's sales and net earnings are also rising.

Some growth investors look at a stock's *momentum* - the highest-flying, hottest, or most aggressive stocks of the moment - to determine picks, and they will pay almost any price to own them, hoping for a *Greater Fool* to sell to later. Such investors - or, should I say, speculators - are willing to ride out the volatility of their favorite "hot" stock for the chance to make a fortune.

More rational growth investors look for GARP - growth at reasonable prices - and will ignore high-flying, momentum stocks if the prices are too steep.[80]

The downside to growth investing is similar to the downside for value investing. The calculations of growth, momentum, or GARP figures relies upon the legitimacy of corporate earnings, sales projections, the company "story," or market share numbers that are published by none other than the companies themselves. Sometimes, market share statistics are available through independent industry market reports, but *earnings* (as we have seen) are the most manipulated numbers in the corporate world.

Additionally, momentum methods carry high (often unacceptable) levels of risk to all but pure gamblers. In my opinion, buying stocks at high "multiples" (P/E ratios) simply because they currently exhibit high growth rates is a recipe for disaster. The growth investing strategy is too often in clear violation of the *Stock Market Mercenary's universal rules* of investing.

---

[79] Warren Buffett, February 28, 1997. "Berkshire Hathaway Inc - Chairman's Letter - 1996" (www.berkshirehathaway.com/letters/1996.html) Used by permission.
[80] Sincere, p. 17.

Quantitative Investing

"Quants" rely heavily on proprietary computer models and quantitative formulae to find the best stocks. This method is a high-tech number crunching game. It is the most "objective" of systems in that Quants rely entirely on the output from their models. The subjective part comes with constant fine-tuning adjustments that must be made to improve the model over time. The overriding goal is to design the perfect computer model that will find the perfect stock at the perfect time. There are a different set of quantitative parameters for every Quant strategist out there, but they all seem to agree on one guideline: the computer will determine which stocks to trade.[81]

This strategy, while sometimes very accurate, relies on extremely complicated criteria, violating the *universal rule* that simple methods are superior. Unless you're willing to invest huge sums of money in another person's quantitative model, you will most likely be unable to participate in this strategy. An alternative to quantitative modeling might be a "hybrid" method that combines statistical analysis and other investment strategies to develop a set of simple rules that are easily executed. Invariably, such a strategy would be immediately labeled a "mechanical system" and would be discredited by the experts.

As a computer professional, I am both fascinated and frustrated with quantitative studies. On the one hand, I enjoy the tangible benefits of technology and its employment to solve real-world problems. On the other, I am frustrated that, sometimes, computers are used by investors who are either unable or unwilling to do the "hard research" necessary to find stocks in the "buy low, sell high" category. A computer, for example, cannot read a long-term chart with the cognitive ease of a human brain and human eyes. This partly explains the exorbitant cost of "quantitative" systems, requiring near artificial intelligence programming to pick worthy stocks from among the 10,000 available (including penny stocks).

Finally, quantitative strategies ignore the last two of our *universal rules*. I haven't found a computer yet that actually "understood" a company's business model or knew intuitively whether a company was a "real wealth creator." If you are either extremely rich, or extremely lazy, then quantitative strategies may be your thing.

Dow or Index Strategies

Index strategies follow the progress of entire groups of stocks, such as the Dow Jones[SM] Top 30 Industrials (a.k.a., the "Dow"), the Standard & Poor 500 Index (a.k.a., the "S&P 500"), the NASDAQ 100, and the Value Line (a group of 1,650 or so of the top companies). Most index investors attempt to simply meet or beat the performance of the Dow or S&P 500 each year. If you believe (as many do) that the Dow and S&P tend to gain every two years out of three, you may also believe that your investments are "safer" than most while still having a decent upside potential. Like the insurance business, index strategies attempt to manage risks by spreading them across a large array of companies.

All it takes is one bad market downturn, however, to undo any profits accumulated by index players. The Tech Bubble is a recent example. The economy was already showing signs of a

---

[81] Sincere, p. 18.

recession from early-2000 through September 10, 2001, and the airlines were already hurting. The stock market was generally trending downward, and that trend was assisted by terrorist attacks (see Figure 4-1). On September 10th, the Dow opened at 9,603.40, compared to its high of 11,908.50 on January 14, 2000 - a 20 percent decline to that point. Rather than hit the usual yearly lows in late October, the Dow reached a dismal 7,926.90 on September 21st - ten days after the attacks - losing an additional 17 percent within eleven days. Many Index Fund players lost their shirts during this period.

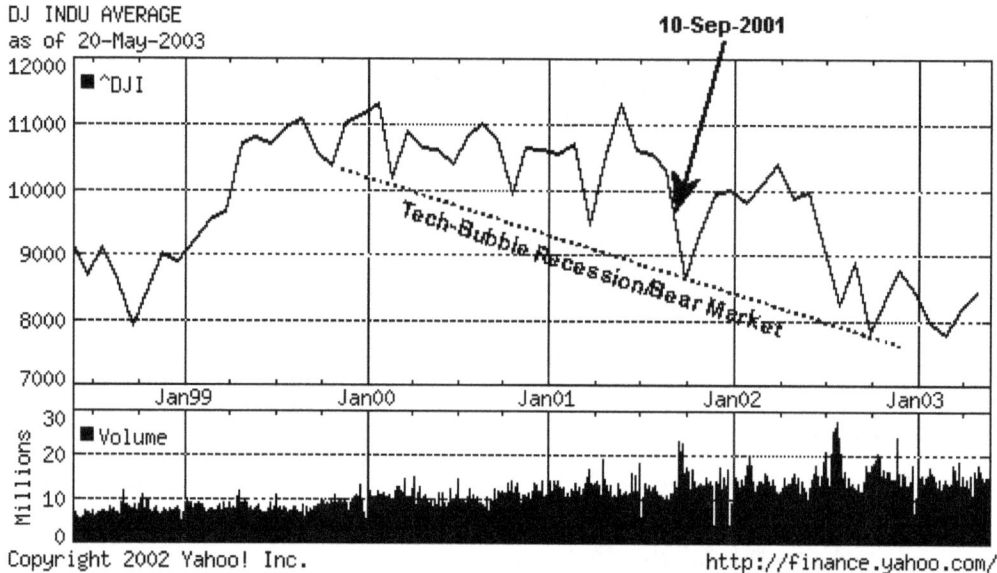

FIGURE 4-1. Dow Jones[SM] **Industrial Average showing the post-Tech-Bubble Recession period. (Trend line and notations added by author.)** [Reproduced with permission of Yahoo! Inc. © 2003 by Yahoo! Inc. YAHOO! and the YAHOO! logo are trademarks of Yahoo! Inc.]

Did these events have anything whatsoever to do with the actual health of the thirty industrial companies that comprise the Dow? Those components involved in high-tech and dot-com ventures had already been "punished" for their earlier indulgences, so the Dow was acting "normally" prior to the terrorist acts. The point is that index strategies often require one eye on the market and the other eye on geopolitical intelligence to discern market direction.

One popular strategy, advocated by "The Motley Fool,"[82] an entertaining and informative Internet advisory group dedicated to the survival of "Fool-ish" investors, is their latest revision of "The Foolish Four" approach.[83] Once each year, you rank all 30 Dow stocks by dividing their annual dividend yields by the square root of their stock prices, sorting them from highest to lowest result. Then, you discard the top-ranked stock and buy an equal dollar amount of the next highest four stocks. Near the end of each year, you adjust your portfolio, selling stocks no longer qualified and buying new ones that are. Over the past 25 years, this method has produced better than 24 percent average annual returns.

Another long-held Dow strategy, described by Michael Sincere (and many others), is to simply pick the ten highest dividend-yielding Dow stocks and to hold them for one year,

---

[82] The Motley Fool (www.fool.com)
[83] The Motley Fool, 1998. "Dow Investing Explained." (www.fool.com/school/dowinvesting.htm)

repeating the process each year.[84] Also known as the "Dogs of the Dow" method, this popular strategy has averaged about 17 percent in each of the past 25 years, but with higher risk than other strategies. Very often in the Dow, high dividend payers tend to be lower-priced (or out-of-favor) stocks, hence the "dog" label. Thus, if all ten candidates are truly "dogs," your risk is lower; but a few high-priced, high-yield stocks in the kennel can raise your risk considerably.

For those wishing to spread their risk over a broader group of stocks, the S&P 500 and Value Line indexes offer reasonable returns in most years, usually in the 12 to 20 percent range.

As we have discussed, the downside to virtually all index strategies is that they are subject to "macro" manipulations, economic downturns, catastrophes, wars, and other events that affect the emotions of the public and are out of the public's control. While these risks are very real, there are methods designed to dramatically lower some of the risks and improve annual yields.

If you are capable of extreme discipline and understand the value of sound money management, you can use leverage to make a consistent profit with index funds by buying them as futures contracts on the commodities market. This is risky, but has much higher potential returns to offset that risk. We will cover one such strategy later.

Contrarian Investing

Hetty Green died in 1916 the richest woman in America, and among the top twenty richest people in the world. Hetty was a miser's miser, and would expend many days of effort to save a few cents, or to simply prevent the need to spend money, but she was considered a genius at making money. Her mantra, "buy cheap and sell dear," has become the watchword of *Contrarians* everywhere. It takes a lot of discipline to consistently go against the popular trends, and to ignore the advice offered by today's investment professionals, but the most successful *Stock Market Mercenaries* within the last century have been - for the most part - *Contrarians*. Most institutional traders are *Contrarian*, and since they make a profit most of the time, and the public loses most of the time, it is clear which philosophy is superior.

A true *Contrarian* looks for companies that are temporarily out of favor and are underperforming the market. *Contrarians* love companies that others (including Wall Street "gurus") hate, but that exhibit superior prospects for future growth. *Contrarians* pay close attention to psychological factors, and they believe that there is a "follow-the-herd" mentality among the majority of traders. When stocks have been slammed because investors panicked or overreacted, the *Contrarian* steps in and buys. Companies with extremely low P/E ratios, and even those with (temporarily) *negative* earnings are candidates for *Contrarian* investing.[85]

To be a successful *Contrarian*, you must have control of your emotions and must be willing to go against the crowd. You will buy stocks that few others would even consider, and will sell when everyone in Wall Street, it seems, is buying. John D. Rockefeller is credited with the rather cynical *Contrarian* quote: "The way to make money is to buy when blood is running in the streets." Of course, it only sounds "cynical" to those who bought at the top!

The downside to *Contrarian* investing is that, in the course of seeking stocks that are at the bottom, and that nobody wants, you may occasionally buy one that is too far-gone and actually does go under. Great care should be taken to ensure that the company is not "dead" - just

---

[84] Sincere, pp. 18-19.
[85] Sincere, pp. 17-18.

"unloved" for now. Negative earnings reports are no problem, and manipulated corporate financial statements are mostly irrelevant to *Contrarians*, because these instruments are published to influence the "herd," while *Contrarians* do the opposite. As we will see in the next chapter, there are ways to distinguish between a dying company and a temporarily-unloved company.

Chartists

A "chartist" is a technical investor (having a largely mechanical method) who relies on long-term charts to uncover patterns that, historically, indicate trading opportunities. For instance, many chartists believe that corporate insiders and institutional traders buy and sell in predictable patterns designed to fool (or manipulate) the public into doing the opposite; and that these patterns are easily identified on long-term stock price charts. Once the patterns are identified, the chartist can make trades that mimic the actions of the insiders, buying when they do (at or near the bottom) and selling when they do (at or near the top). In that sense, chartists are very much like *Contrarians*, except that they use charts as their primary input.

Some chartist methods, however, are extremely short-term in nature, relying on the past few days or weeks to form telltale patterns. Such methods do not assume that a stock's lifetime history will indicate the potential of the stock. Instead, they rely simply on recent "wiggle-waggles" of price action to guide the chartist's actions. For example, many day traders use "candlestick" charts showing the previous few days' price patterns to determine today's trades. Never mind that the reason a stock goes up or down today may be as a result of manipulation, war, terrorism, oil prices, panic, or over-hyped marketing.

Chartists, for the most part, ignore corporate financial statements (a.k.a., "fundamentals"), market headlines, major economic events, advice from brokers and analysts, and (especially) TV commentators. To many chartists, only the potential effect of this information on the public psychology is considered. Since the charts most likely used by the public are short-term (one year or less), the public will be easily duped into participating in short-term speculation, while the long-term chartist - armed with the "big picture" - takes profitable advantage.

The downside to the chartist philosophy is that, like the *Contrarian* strategies, ignoring all fundamentals can sometimes lead to the purchase of stocks in companies too near death to recover. Using a few objective numbers, however, can help prevent these mistakes, if only to *validate* the picks chosen from the charts.

Finally, no matter how well designed a chartist strategy is, and no matter how well it is managed, it's very existence flies in the face of a government-imposed "orthodoxy" (supported by most business schools) bent upon discrediting any technical system.

Stock Charts and the Federal "Gag Order"

Some of the most consistently profitable stock trading methods I have encountered - and validated through years of statistical back-testing, paper-trading, and real capital - have been based largely on a combination of Chartist and *Contrarian* philosophies. In fact, some very successful methods rely heavily on long-term charts to disclose the patterns that expose manipulation by institutional investors. Could it be that institutional traders do not want the public to uncover these patterns? Is it possible that the Federal Government, through the Securities and Exchange Commission, is protecting institutional investors by discrediting any method that relies upon price charts or objective formulas that might expose the manipulation we have documented? Figure 4-2 reveals the text of a current SEC regulation that ties the hands of investment professionals, preventing them from advocating any such trading method without also discrediting that method.

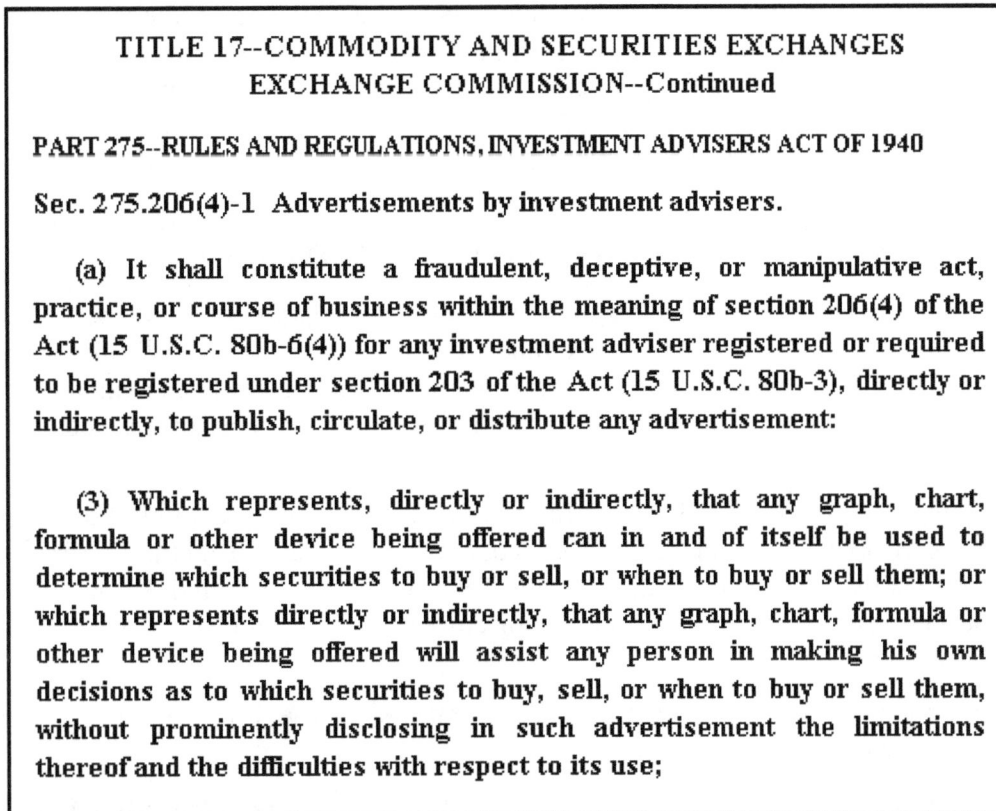

**TITLE 17--COMMODITY AND SECURITIES EXCHANGES
EXCHANGE COMMISSION--Continued**

PART 275--RULES AND REGULATIONS, INVESTMENT ADVISERS ACT OF 1940

Sec. 275.206(4)-1 Advertisements by investment advisers.

(a) It shall constitute a fraudulent, deceptive, or manipulative act, practice, or course of business within the meaning of section 206(4) of the Act (15 U.S.C. 80b-6(4)) for any investment adviser registered or required to be registered under section 203 of the Act (15 U.S.C. 80b-3), directly or indirectly, to publish, circulate, or distribute any advertisement:

(3) Which represents, directly or indirectly, that any graph, chart, formula or other device being offered can in and of itself be used to determine which securities to buy or sell, or when to buy or sell them; or which represents directly or indirectly, that any graph, chart, formula or other device being offered will assist any person in making his own decisions as to which securities to buy, sell, or when to buy or sell them, without prominently disclosing in such advertisement the limitations thereof and the difficulties with respect to its use;

FIGURE 4-2. SEC Regulation establishing a de facto "gag order" against any investment method utilizing graphs, charts or formulas. SOURCE: Securities and Exchange Commission (www.sec.gov).

Note that in this regulation, graphs, charts and formulas cannot be offered as the *sole* source of picking or timing stock trades, *nor* can graphs, charts and formulas be offered to merely *assist* you in picking or timing your stock trades, without also offering the "limitations" and "difficulties" of these tools. Of course, this regulation *assumes* that, no matter how effective and reliable - no matter how simple, no matter how well-proven - the graph, chart or formula in question **must** be represented to the public as "limited" and "difficult."

This regulation is tantamount to a federal "gag order," which discredits - or limits exposure to - any legitimate technical or chartist method, no matter how successfully the method performs. In large part, this regulation answers the question: "Why do investment professionals and TV analysts advocate only those methods to the public that rely upon company fundamentals?" Could it be that the "bad advice" (discussed in previous chapters) given to the public is a direct result of this federal gag order?

Finally, did you notice that little gem in *subparagraph (3)* about offering persons graphs, charts or formulas that would assist them in making their *own* trading decisions? **Are members of the public somehow too stupid to make up their own minds about which stocks to buy or**

sell and when to buy or sell them? Are members of the public incapable of determining for themselves the usefulness of graphs, charts and formulas in the pursuit of stock market profits? Evidently the SEC believes the answer to both questions is "yes."

I have already shown how the government taxes and inflates away our capital, and how it allows its bankruptcy courts to assist fraudulent public companies in their schemes against creditors and shareholders. Now, we see that the government is a party to the actual manipulation of the advice offered to the public, by labeling the mere advocacy of a technical trading method as "fraudulent, deceptive, or manipulative." So much for freedom of speech! The real market manipulators must be powerful indeed, to have such government support for their actions.

Finding the Most Profitable Methods

For the past seven years, my colleagues and I at *Larkin Industries* have been statistically analyzing over 70 leading stock and index fund trading methods, derived from every strategy discussed in this chapter. Of course, there are hundreds of trading methods available today, but we selected the ones with the most "ink" in the media, the best-sellers, or the ones earning the most public "chatter" on the Internet.

Part of our analysis included back-testing the methods against real market data from 1930 forward, in an effort to prove them in good economies and bad. All methods were especially "stressed" against the crashes of 1962, 1987, the Tech Bubble of 2000, and the post-9/11 market (each labeled by revisionist historians as "major corrections") to validate whether the methods remained profitable.

For a trading method to "survive" the statistical analysis phase, it had to meet or exceed any three of the following four **primary goals**:

1. **Method is profitable in at least nine (9) years out of any consecutive ten (10) year period.**

2. **Method's average annual profits are, after deducting capital gains taxes, in excess of the capital erosion caused by the actual inflation rate during any given test period.**

3. **Method was profitable during the Depression (early 30's), and the years 1962, 1987, and the period 2000 through 2002.**

4. **Method equals or outperforms the S&P 500 Index during good economic years, and at least breaks even (after taxes and inflation) during bad economic years.**

Sadly, I must report that **none** of the methods met all four primary goals in every year tested. Happily, I can report that a few of the methods outperformed the others by a wide margin, earning worthwhile profits *almost* every year, during any economy, during periods of geopolitical turmoil, in bull markets and bear markets, while being virtually immune to market manipulation and accounting irregularities.

Those few surviving methods were then subjected to further tests to determine if they met any of the following eight **secondary goals**:

1. **Method *assumes* stocks (and/or the public) are in fact routinely manipulated, or it *allows* for that possibility.**

2. **Method uncovers the signals that the manipulators are making a move.**

3. **Method uncovers *when* the manipulators are making a move.**

4. **Method relies the *least* on corporate financial statements (fundamentals), which are subject to manipulation.**

5. **Method provides multiple indicators to validate a particular stock pick.**

6. **Method minimizes risks by picking stocks that are at historically low prices.**

7. **Method is *simple* to actually implement by non-professional traders.**

8. **Method requires no emotional, and very little subjective, input to determine the worthiness of a particular stock.**

Each method was rigorously tested in both large and small portfolios, with stocks of large and small companies. Some methods were subjected to more than 100,000 simulated trades over a 72-year period. **Of all the popular investing methods we tested, nine were statistically profitable, if used exactly as prescribed by their authors.** The definition of "statistically profitable" was simply "able to keep up with inflation and capital gains taxes," which may or may not be *sufficiently profitable!*[86] Even some of these "winners" were inconsistent, losing money in a few of the years tested, but doing quite well in other years to stay in-the-black overall.

While our statistical back-testing was relatively straight-forward, the more subjective methods required considerable care in setting up the business rules to simulate human judgment on our computers. These judgments were approximated by building "reasonable ranges" of tolerance to the stock-picking decision process. While not as precise as the human brain, the technique had the benefit of being relatively consistent. Of course, one cannot expect perfection from subjective decisions - whether by computer or by human!

Our analysis clearly illustrated that a method's risk increased proportionately with its level of complexity, meaning that the risks of more complicated methods far outweighed their potential for profit, rendering them useless. If we then applied certain modifications to these methods, resulting in higher profits or lower risks, we accepted them as modified. Otherwise, they were discarded.

Of the nine "statistically profitable" methods, all met at least *four* of our eight secondary goals. We discovered that each of these winning methods could be improved upon with minor modifications or better research techniques. Only our top choice required no modifications to be consistently profitable, however, we were still able to increase its profits and lower the risks with our modifications.

Starting with the method showing the *least* risk, the three "winners" were:

1. Ted Warren's "Investolator®" method, from his book, *How To Make the Stock Market Make Money For You* (1998, 3ʳᵈ edition, The Ted Warren Corporation, Grants Pass, OR, 541-955-2779). The original version was published in 1966 but had limited circulation. **This method met nearly all of our requirements, showed the least risk, and was consistently profitable, with annual portfolio returns ranging from 6 to 136 percent, averaging 67 percent in annual profits (before commissions). Results on individual**

---

[86] At the time of this writing, new tax-cut legislation is pending which may "temporarily" reduce the capital gains and dividend tax rate from 28% to 15%. It is unlikely that this rate will remain that low for long, if history is the "norm."

stock trades, however, exceeded 300 percent on many occasions. We were able to improve the method's performance by adding some risk-reducing steps and better screening processes designed to pick truly "institutionalized" stocks at their prime. The result of these modifications was an increase in overall profits by 10 to 15 percent. The most dramatic improvement, however, was the ability of our tests to disqualify truly bad stocks that would ordinarily have qualified under the original method. We will discuss these modifications in Chapter 5.

2. Larkin Industries' index fund method, the *Leveraged Index Fund Strategy* (2001, Larkin Industries, Inc., Carson City, NV). Of the three winners listed here, this method is the least "exciting," because it only results in two to four trades per year. Those gamblers among you - who like lots of action - will probably pass on this one. *Mercenaries*, on the other hand, will find it profitable and reliable with surprisingly moderate risk. The strategy is derived from the historical fact that the overall market high in most years is reached in the Spring or early Summer, and the "market cycle" low for the year often occurs between mid-September and late-October. **This method met nearly all of our requirements and ranged between losses of 6 percent to gains of 655 percent annually, averaging 92 percent. Within the past ten years, however, the average annual returns exceeded 120 percent.** We will cover this method in Chapter 6.

3. Benjamin Graham's value investing method, from his book, *The Intelligent Investor* (1949, HarperBusiness, New York, NY); a "layman's" version of a 1934 book titled *Security Analysis*, by Benjamin Graham and David Dodd (McGraw-Hill, New York, NY). **This method met many of our requirements but was vulnerable to both price manipulation and misleading accounting practices. Annual returns ranged from losses of 16 percent to gains of 72 percent, averaging 21 percent in annual profits. Unfortunately, this method violated secondary goals 4 and 7, relying primarily on fundamentals and being one of the most complicated and time-consuming methods we tested.** If you can trade stocks for a living, this method will keep you very busy indeed, but will make a reasonable annual return. The amount of effort per dollar earned, however, will be considerably more than the other winning strategies on this list.

You may be asking: if these methods are so successful, why don't more people know about them? The answer is simple. Except for Ben Graham's value investing, the above methods qualify as "fraudulent, deceptive or manipulative" under the SEC's orthodoxy, and must, therefore, be labeled as "difficult" and "limited" pursuant to Sec. 275.206(4)-1(a)(3). Why? Because they rely primarily on charts, graphs, historical patterns and technical indicators to pick and time stock trades. They are also designed to help individual traders pick their *own* stocks – another no-no. Rather than risk sanction by the SEC, licensed market analysts, brokers, and other investment professionals tend to shy away from such strategies. Despite its complexity and time-consuming nature, requiring the assistance of professionals in most cases, Graham's value method relies primarily on fundamental indicators and is, thus, "safe" from SEC ire.

Summary

Of all the popular investment strategies that rely upon corporate fundamentals - financial statements, earnings reports, etc. - value investing, in the capable hands of gurus like Warren Buffett, will produce long-term profits. For the individual public trader, who can neither spare the time and effort to properly calculate a company's intrinsic value, nor entrust his retirement capital to a value fund manager he has never met, the successful alternatives are few.

Stock Market Mercenaries pick strategies from among the *Contrarian* and technical choices, or mix compatible strategies to limit their risks and provide a reasonable and consistent profit. But don't bother asking your broker's opinion about which technical or chartist method he would recommend. The investment industry - with federal backing - does not want him to speak favorably of any such strategy, especially if it is likely to help you make your **own** stock picking decisions.

Despite the media and SEC bias against certain investment philosophies, our research has found solid, proven, low-risk, and relatively-simple approaches capable of Buffett-style returns that would make Hetty Green smile with approval. Your *Mercenary* training continues!

"Let us be thankful for the fools. But for them the rest of us could not succeed."

--Mark Twain

Chapter 5: Profiting on Manipulated Stocks

Ride the coattails of those who move the market

In the previous chapter, I revealed two proven, statistically profitable stock-picking philosophies that met nearly all of the goals set by our testing team at *Larkin Industries*. Unfortunately, one of these winning strategies - value investing - was found to be way too complicated for the average public investor. In fact, it's pretty tough for professional value fund managers as well, since few are able to beat the performance of stock index funds year after year. My primary objection to value investing, however, is its vulnerability to the manipulation of corporate financial statements. Only those with direct access to the internals of a company can truly know its financial health and prospects for future growth. Although value investing is supposed to help us quantify, and, therefore, manage our capital risk, it cannot reliably prevent losses due to misstated financial results. Despite this risk, the method continues to thrive, earning steady profits almost every year.

However, the remaining (non-index-fund) strategy - Ted Warren's *Investolator*® method - survives as our tested winner. Not only did we statistically back-test this method from 1930 forward, we have actively traded it since 1998, in multiple portfolios, with real money, and have achieved significant returns. Many investment strategies are "back-tested," but very few can stand up to actual trading conditions in both good and bad economies, bull and bear markets, or periods of geopolitical turmoil. In fact, many popular stock-picking strategies today are developed by "curve-fitting" their rules into past statistics. Not so with Warren's method. His philosophy was based on his first-hand observation that individual stocks were routinely manipulated, and that this activity was "telegraphed" to savvy chartists, allowing them to simply react to the inevitable profit opportunity, essentially allowing them to ride the coattails of the manipulators.

The Ted Warren Philosophy

I introduced you to Ted Warren in Chapter 3 and discussed his perspective on the influence of "mob psychology" on the average investor. Then, in Chapter 4, we discussed *Contrarian* and Chartist strategies. The *Investolator* method is a hybrid strategy using long-term charts to uncover the machinations of stock manipulators, basing trading decisions upon the *opposite* of the public's anticipated actions. It is from the public's own psychology that this method derives its profit for *Contrarians*.

Fortunately, one does not need a degree in psychology to know what the "natural" human reactions are to news headlines and certain price movements. For that, we have over 185 years of U.S. stock market history to back up Warren's theories. His method is one of the few strategies revealing stock-buying opportunities at historical bottoms, thereby reducing investment risk and maximizing potential profit. Where one *sells* the stock is a bit more subjective, and dependent upon your goals, but the key to locking in future profits is buying at the bottom - before the "hot" rally begins.

Like value investors, Warren attempted to find under-priced stocks and make low-risk trades. Unlike value investors, he usually bought those same stocks at lower prices, and sold them when the uptrend was broken, rather than holding them for long periods. One of the most important differences between these strategies is the ease with which Warren's method uncovers opportunities. Instead of gathering up to 250 data points, calculating dozens of ratios, and running background checks on a company's management team, we can rely on signals provided by the institutional traders and corporate insiders themselves to time our trades. Many of those signals can be found on long-term charts. Others are freely available on the Internet, a technology that wasn't around in Ted Warren's day.

The purpose of this chapter is not to parrot a complete lesson on the late Ted Warren's method, especially since it is thoroughly documented in his 305-page book, *How To Make the Stock Market Make Money for You*.[87] However, since this is the most successful individual stock-picking method we tested, and since our tests benefited from some important modifications to validate each trade and further reduce risk, my intention is to describe the salient points of *my version* of the strategy, and allow you to learn the core principles from Warren's book, including the proper interpretation of a long-term stock chart. Not that the chart itself can predict what direction the stock will go, but that it clearly reveals the actions of those who control the lion's share of the stock. Thus, the method is "reactionary" to the patterns and trends revealed in the charts.

While this method is not very complicated, it does require that you completely rethink any other strategy. For example, I have yet to find a broker, analyst, or accountant willing to acknowledge that manipulation commonly exists in the stock market. Are they uninformed, in denial, or simply deflecting their own cynical role in the scam? I don't know the answer, but, once they have seen my personal results from the method, their eyes widen to near anatomically-impossible sizes.

Later in this chapter, you will see descriptions and charts of a handful of my past trades, marked with my entry and exit points. All of these trades are real, and can be verified with brokerage trade confirmation statements. Note the similarities of the price patterns and daily volume patterns on the charts leading up to my trades. Combined with institutional and insider trading statistics from the Internet, the charts are a formidable tool for *Mercenaries*.

In past years, obtaining the charts and research data required for prudent stock selection was both difficult and time-consuming. In most cases, by the time you could see a chart, it was too late to act. Now, with the Internet Age (one beneficial outcome of the "technological bubble"), all the information you need to be a successful stock trader is readily available - for free - online.

The best way to explain how I pick stocks using this method is to literally "show and tell." I will, therefore, take you step-by-step through the thought process I use to select and time my trades.

---

[87] Ted Warren, 1966. "How To Make the Stock Market Make Money For You" (The Ted Warren Corporation, Grants Pass, OR, 541-955-2779, 3rd edition, 1998).

The Picking and Trading Process

The overriding principle is, of course, to buy low and sell high. In practice, this is easier said than done. I use online "stock screeners" to find good leads on potential bargains. My favorite screeners are at *Yahoo! Finance* (http://finance.yahoo.com), or at some of the online brokerage websites - the former is free, the latter requires an active trading account. The best screening tools will include filters for institutional and insider ownership percentages. This is merely a time-saver, helping you quickly weed out stocks that the institutions and insiders are not presently accumulating. For the sake of brevity, except where indicated, I will use the term "insiders" to represent both corporate insiders and institutional investors. The term "manipulators" is used to include all the players in the investment industry capable of moving a stock's price or influencing the public to act a certain way.

Step 1 - Find "Unloved" Stocks

Stocks nobody wants eventually end up at the bottom, where they can remain for a long period (sometimes three, four or more years). If manipulation is occurring, you will see over time a steady increase in ownership by the insiders. Once they have accumulated most of the stock, they will "allow" it to be distributed to the gullible public at much-higher prices. Of course, to mask the fact that the insiders are accumulating a stock, you might see negative headlines, or no headlines at all, during the accumulation period - usually while the price is at historical lows. Thus, if the public is to read *anything* about the stock at this time, it will be decidedly negative. Should word get out that the insiders are lapping up every share they can, it would start a premature rally.

Another way the manipulators discourage the public is by using short-term false rallies. For example, if a stock price has been going sideways at the bottom for many months, and then, suddenly, spikes upward, the public may think that the "rally" is finally here, and will start buying. Often, the price will later drop to a point *below* the recent support levels, inducing the public to sell out. Others, who might have been tempted to buy, are now completely disgusted with the stock and lose interest. Often, this scenario motivates existing shareholders to finally part with their long-held shares. As soon as these last few shares have been transferred to the insiders, giving them the "corner" on the market, the *true* rally can begin. Our goal is to catch the insiders in the act of cornering stocks.

If your online stock screener has an "Institutional Ownership" filter, start by narrowing your search to companies with at least 60 percent of the stock currently owned by institutions. **A stock that rallies without high institutional ownership is likely not being manipulated.** There are exceptions. For example, corporate insiders who own stock are not considered "institutional" traders, thus their percentage ownership is a separate number. If your stock screener has a separate "Insider Ownership" filter, you're in luck. After you've studied the stocks chosen from the Institutional search, perform your next search on companies whose "Insider Ownership" is at least 40 percent. If either search returns no companies, then lower your percentage and repeat the search, until you do get some stocks. If your search returns more than 20 stocks, raise the percentage and repeat the search. The higher the ownership, the "riper" the stock is for the picking.

If your online stock screener has neither institutional nor insider filters, start by picking all stocks with P/E (price-to-earnings) ratios of 9 or less. Most such stocks are out of favor. You may end up with hundreds of symbols. If so, you can also select a negative earnings or a decline in sales as additional "out-of-favor" filters. Actually, we don't really care which "fundamental" causes a stock to be "unloved."

From among your candidates, find the longest-term, linear[88] chart for each stock symbol and look for the classic pattern. For example, in late-March 2002, I found the following chart (Figure 5-1) for "Brass Eagle" (XTRM), a paintball supply firm, with a P/E ratio of 8.85. Brass Eagle's long-term chart indicated a recognizable opportunity (Ted Warren's book is the "bible" of chartist technique, and will clearly define what a "recognizable opportunity" is).

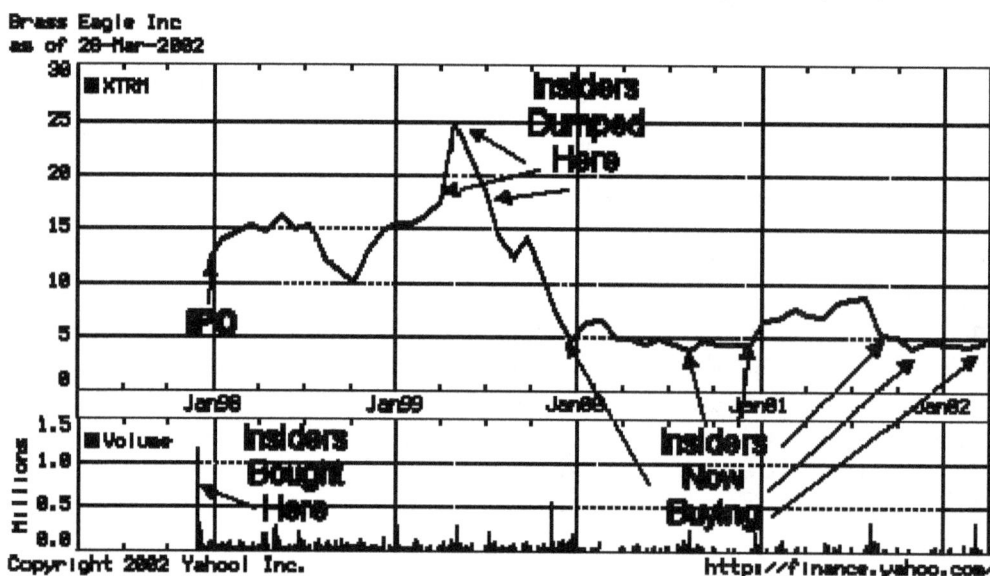

FIGURE 5-1. Brass Eagle (XTRM) - Long-term Chart. (Marks added) [Reproduced with permission of Yahoo! Inc. © 2003 by Yahoo! Inc. YAHOO! and the YAHOO! logo are trademarks of Yahoo! Inc.]

Step 2 - Verify Insider and Institutional Ownership

It is important to verify that the stock has high insider and/or institutional ownership. Why? Because, if they are just beginning to accumulate shares, you may have to wait a few years before you see a rally. The key is patience - wait until they have most of the shares, then jump aboard. While Ted Warren used certain price and volume chart patterns to determine the readiness of a stock to rally, I prefer more empirical numbers to back up my interpretation of the chart.

If you are using *Yahoo! Finance*, click on the "Profile" link (usually located below the chart) to see what percentage ownership the manipulators have. In the case of Brass Eagle, I found the following statistics on the *Yahoo! Finance* Profile page:

---

[88] Yahoo!'s online charts come in two flavors: "log" and "linear." A "log" chart is weighted and doesn't show the price marks at equal intervals, but shrinks the scale as the price increases. This tends to distort the price pattern. A "linear" chart shows the true picture of historical price action, and doesn't "bias" the pattern.

Ownership

- **Insider and 5%+ Owners:** 64%
- Over the last 6 months:
  - one insider buy; 1,000 shares
- **Institutional:** 72% (197% of float) (29 institutions)
- **Net Inst. Buying:** 127.0K shares (+2.42%) (prior quarter to latest quarter)

FIGURE 5-2. Insider and Institutional ownership statistics for XTRM. [Reproduced with permission of Yahoo! Inc. © 2003 by Yahoo! Inc. YAHOO! and the YAHOO! logo are trademarks of Yahoo! Inc.]

The "Ownership" statistics shown can sometimes be confusing due to overlapping figures. Note that, in Figure 5-2, the total of Insider and Institutional ownership appears to be 136 percent! Actually, the "Insider and 5%+ Owners" number includes both corporate officers and anybody else who has at least five percent of the shares, *including institutions*. Meanwhile, if any of those "5% Owners" happens to be an institution, it will also be included in the "Institutional" total. This gives the impression that insiders and institutions can own more than 100 percent of all the stock. To resolve the problem, just click on the underlined "institutions" link in parentheses to see a list of the top institutions. For Brass Eagle, I found a long list of institutions, but only *two* with at least five percent of the stock (see the "%Out" column in Figure 5-3).

Ownership Information - Brass Eagle Inc (NasdaqNM:XTRM) **As of 30-Mar-02**

Top Institutional Fund Holders	Shares	%Out*	Value**	Reported
Charter Oak Partners	3,674,474	51.41	$15,432,790	30-Sep-01
Dimensional Fund Advisors Inc	527,900	7.38	$2,217,180	30-Sep-01

FIGURE 5-3. Top Institutional Fund Holders of XTRM. [Reproduced with permission of Yahoo! Inc. © 2003 by Yahoo! Inc. YAHOO! and the YAHOO! logo are trademarks of Yahoo! Inc.]

The total shares held by "5% Owners" is 4.2 million. Near the bottom of *Yahoo!'s* "Profile" page (not shown) is the total number of "Shares Outstanding," or 7.15 million. Since the total "Insider" ownership is 64 percent, multiplying by 7.15 million shares, we get 4.576 million. Subtracting the "5% Owners" (4.2 million), we get 376,000 shares held by *non-institutional* insiders. We also know that 72 percent of all shares are held by institutions, so 5.148 million shares less 4.2 million (5% Owners) leaves 948,000 shares held by all other institutional traders. Thus, we can calculate the ownership as follows:

XTRM, Total Shares Outstanding	7,150,000	100.00%
Insiders (officers & directors)	376,000	5.30%
Institutions with 5% or higher	4,200,000	58.70%
Other Institutions/Mutual Funds	948,000	13.30%
Total:	5,524,000	77.30%

FIGURE 5-4. Calculating the total insider and institutional ownership.

So, as of March 30, 2002, at least 77 percent of all Brass Eagle shares were being held by insiders and institutions. Further, according to the "Ownership" summary on *Yahoo's* Profile page (Figure 5-2), the institutions were still buying, another indicator that accumulation was afoot. You may have noticed that some of the institutional ownership figures for XTRM were current as of the previous quarter. A lot could have happened in the months since that report. By clicking on the "Insiders" link on the *Yahoo* Profile page, however, you can see the most recent trades by both insiders and "beneficial owners." If they are still buying, then your ownership calculations will be "conservative." If the big rally hasn't started yet, you still have time to hop on the train before it leaves the station.

The point of this exercise is to determine how close the manipulators are to "cornering" the market on Brass Eagle. When they think they have enough to control the price, they will send it up - hopefully, with their coattails firmly in our grasp. I usually find that the "big move" starts after they have accumulated at least 80 percent of the stock. I've been wrong, of course. Sometimes they send it sooner!

Step 3 - Make Sure Insiders Aren't Looting the Cash

Ted Warren basically ignored any fundamentals, especially those derived from a company's financial statements.[89] While I fully agree that financial statements are irrelevant to stock price manipulation, except to mislead the public, there are times when a stock is at the bottom because it is being looted of its cash, a tell-tale sign that the company may be going under. Manipulation is one thing - *fraud* is something else!

The signals of such looting can be found from just three numbers in a company's cash-flow statement and balance sheet. To avoid being victimized in the tradition of Priceline.com and Enron, just calculate our *Truth Ratio* to find out if anything stinks.

To find these numbers on *Yahoo! Finance*, just click on the "Financials" link (also under the stock chart), then pick the "Cash Flow" and the "Balance Sheet" tabs to see the figures. The formula for calculating this ratio was described in Chapter 3 ("Priceline.com Saga" section). Just subtract the net change in cash from net income, then divide the result by the total assets. Figure 5-5 is an abbreviated snapshot of the key numbers for Brass Eagle, captured during my research of the stock.

---

[89] Warren, p. 151.

Financials - Brass Eagle Inc (NasdaqNM:XTRM)   **As of 26-Mar-2002**

Cash Flow Statement				
Period Ending:	Sep 30, 2001	Jun 30, 2001	Mar 31, 2001	Dec 31, 2000
Net Income	($418,000)	$1,177,000	$1,308,000	$4,297,000
Change in Cash And Cash Equivalents	($395,000)	($293,000)	($2,338,000)	$3,335,000

Balance Sheet				
Period Ending:	Sep 30, 2001	Jun 30, 2001	Mar 31, 2001	Dec 31, 2000
Total Assets	$90,317,000	$87,997,000	$87,435,000	$95,816,000

FIGURE 5-5. The numbers needed to calculate the Truth Ratio. [Reproduced with permission of Yahoo! Inc. © 2003 by Yahoo! Inc. YAHOO! and the YAHOO! logo are trademarks of Yahoo! Inc.]

Based upon the Truth Ratio formula, for the four quarters shown above, I calculated 0.03%, 1.67%, 4.17% and 1.00%, respectively. It appeared that there were some heavier-than-normal cash manipulations in the first quarter of 2001, but still within acceptable limits (under 10%). Thus, in March 2002, it appeared that Brass Eagle had no skeletons in its closet (unless you count paintball casualties).

Step 4 - Validate Your Buy Price and Timing

Determining your buy price and timing your purchase can often be subjective tasks, but I have found a method that seems to work. In his day, Ted Warren used straight "market orders" (whatever the current price is, that's what you pay). With electronic trading today, market orders make it too easy to get burned by day-traders and brokers who watch every pending order and pounce on suckers (such as public traders who use market orders). I use only "limit orders" which guarantee a purchase price no higher than what I want to pay, which is usually a price near the one paid recently by insiders.

One way to determine the price being paid by insiders is to study the "Insider" page, again on *Yahoo! Finance*. For example, there was very little recent insider trading for Brass Eagle in March 2002, but there was a 1,000-share purchase by one of the company's Directors, Robert P. Sarrazin, on December 7, 2001. He paid $4.24 per share at the time. Of course, Mr. Sarrazin expects to make a profit at that price, and since he is an "insider," he would very likely know how and when such a profit would be realized. On March 30, 2002, when I looked up XTRM, the most recent trading range for the stock had been between $4.20 and $4.80, and, since the possibility existed that the insiders were not finished accumulating shares, there was a chance the price would come down a bit. However, it was not likely to sink much below the price that Mr. Sarrazin had paid three months earlier.

The rule I use is: never chase the stock - make those day-traders chase *my* price. Of course, sometimes this causes me to wait for months to get the price I want, but - more often than not - I eventually get my price. For this example, I assumed that $4.20 to $4.50 was a fair price range. Since I had established that the insiders owned *at least* 77 percent of the stock, it was very likely that Brass Eagle would not have to wait too much longer to be sent upward. Further, this stock had been at, or near historical lows since December 2000, interrupted by a brief rally to $10 in the summer of 2001.

The question is: *once you know what price you're willing to pay, when do you make the trade?*

Ted Warren's timing strategy was simple. He waited for the stock to "break out" of its current trading range before buying. If it broke out *below* the range, he assumed the insiders had a lot more accumulating to do. If it broke out *above* the range (or prior point of resistance), then it was ready to rally if other indicators were present.[90]

Another Warren timing indicator was the trading volume of the stock. If a stock had been at the bottom for a long time, and suddenly the volume became very "quiet," meaning very few shares were traded for a few days or weeks, chances are that the insiders owned all the shares they were going to get. Since no more shares were being offered for sale, there was no reason to keep the price down.

One thing is clear: you should not buy while a stock is still in a downtrend (you can't catch a falling knife). Wait for it to bottom out and go sideways, indicating that the insiders have found the price they are willing to pay. During this period, most of the headlines about the stock will be negative, or neutral at best, and the price action itself will move in a manner designed to "discourage" the public from owning it. Of course, *Mercenaries* are *encouraged* by a *discouraged* public!

Therefore, you can wait until the stock breaks above recent resistance, buying it near that price; or you can wait for the trading volume to drop off and hope there are some shares left. Or, you can do what I do: try to beat the insiders at their own game by waiting until they own 80 percent (or so) of all the stock, and then discover the typical price range they have paid for shares, using limit orders to match that price range. If I end up missing the train, so be it. The nice thing about this method is that there are always new trains headed your way.

Continuing our case study, since the last major resistance point for Brass Eagle was around $10, and current prices were now in the mid-$4.00 range, *and* I had clear evidence that insiders were buying at this level, *and* I knew that only 20 percent of the stock was still available, I did not wait around. In life, there are three kinds of people: those who *make* things happen, those who *watch* things happen, and those who *wonder* what happened.

Step 5 - Buy and Hold Until Your Sell Target is Reached

Whichever timing or pricing variation you choose, the object is to acquire stock at the lowest price, or the price at which your risk is minimal. Rather than a lengthy discourse on what constitutes a "low risk" price, **suffice it to say that a stock purchased at - or near - historical lows, in a company that is owned primarily by those who know the truth about it, and in a company whose cash is not being looted by its officers, is as close to a drop-dead sure thing as you will find in the stock market!**

So, on April Fools Day, 2002, I visited my online broker's website and placed a limit order for 200 shares of Brass Eagle (XTRM) at $4.50 per share. At the time my order was confirmed, the current price was around $4.80. I didn't have to wait long. On April 4th, my order was filled at

---

[90] Warren, p. 17.

$4.50 (the low for the day was $4.40). This was a fortunate fill for me, because the price did not go that low again! My commission was $9.99.

In most cases, I like to set a net profit target of 100 percent. Yes, you read that correctly! My goal is to double the investment on stock trades. Since my investment in Brass Eagle was 909.99, including commission, my desired return would be twice that amount, or $1,819.98. Of course, when I sold the stock, I would be charged another commission, plus any SEC transaction fees (about 3 one-thousandths of a percent), so the estimated gross return would be about $1,830. Dividing by the total number of shares, I found my potential selling price to be $9.15. At this point, there was nothing more to do but wait.

Waiting for the right selling price is the toughest part of any stock trade, because it requires patience and discipline. As a few of my early trades indicate (later in this chapter), I have sold too early on more than one occasion, missing out on some extremely large returns. My returns were good, just not "huge" in those cases. If you are fiscally "conservative" like me, you will often be tempted to take profits early. But, I have found that holding too long – which is usually motivated by greed – can be far worse.

Step 6 - Never Sell Too Late

Sell when you've reached your profit target, or the uptrend is broken. You may have heard the saying, "The trend is your friend to the end." More to the point, if the current price exceeds your profit target, and the uptrend has not been broken, you are in the best of worlds! If the price has not reached your target, but the uptrend is broken, chances are you have made a reasonable profit anyway. Now is not the time to let greed prevent you from locking in your profits.

Being a conservative (or cautious) investor, I tend to sell early more often than other trend-followers. Perhaps it's a sign of aging that makes me panic when I've reached my 100-percent goal and feel compelled to dump my stock. Or, perhaps it's because I'm too lazy to draw a trend line on a chart to see if it has been broken. Regardless, the easiest timing method I have found for selling a stock is to sell at, or above, my profit target. Some brokerages allow you to place a "trailing stop" order on your stock, which automatically raises the price at which the stock is sold as long as the market price continues to rise. For example, once the price exceeds my target, I will occasionally place a trailing stop at a "gap" one or two percent below the current price. The longer the rally lasts, the smaller I make the gap, thus protecting as much of my profits as possible while not requiring that I become a "day-trader" in order to manage the investment.

The simplest technique - and one I use quite often - is to wait until the market price reaches 90 percent of my profit target, and then place a limit order to sell at (or slightly above) my target price. Should the rally continue, I would not benefit from any additional profits, but my minimum profit goal would be guaranteed (assuming the price goes that high).

A more complicated, but purely mechanical, uptrend-following method is to track the past 10 days' price ranges, concentrating on each day's **low**. Then, if today's low is lower than the lowest low of the past ten days, it indicates a "break" of the uptrend, which is the signal to sell. But, frankly, it's much easier to just sell at your profit target!

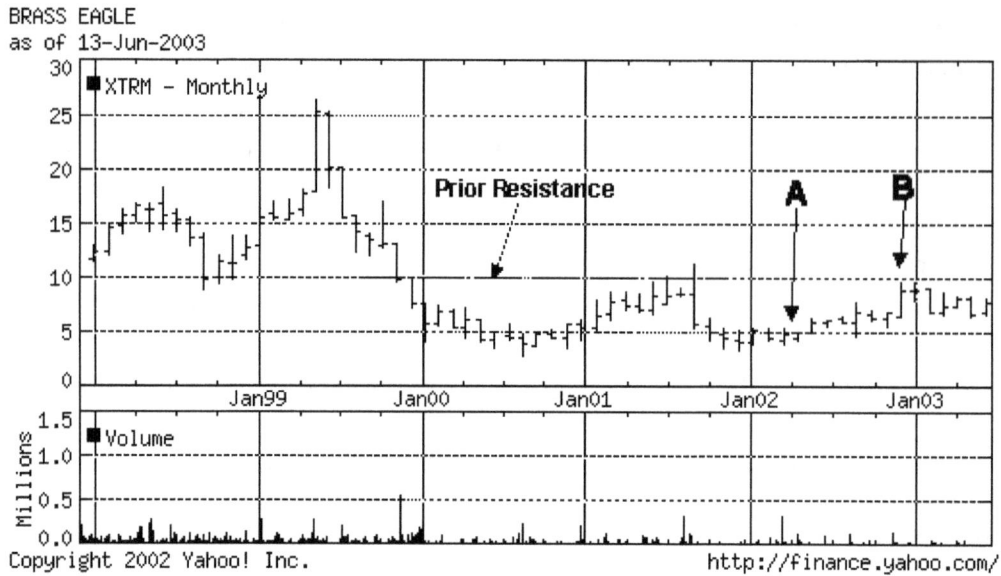

FIGURE 5-6. Brass Eagle (XTRM) buy and sell points. (Marks added.) [Reproduced with permission of Yahoo! Inc. © 2003 by Yahoo! Inc. YAHOO! and the YAHOO! logo are trademarks of Yahoo! Inc.]

Figure 5-6 illustrates what happened with my Brass Eagle investment. Point "A" was my purchase at $4.50 per share on April 4, 2002. On November 8th, the market closed at $8.34, which was within 10 percent of my target price of $9.15. After market hours, I placed an order to sell all 200 shares at $9.25. Granted, this was a price below the "resistance" mark set the previous summer. The likelihood of XTRM continuing to rally well beyond this point was good. However, another visit to *Yahoo! Finance* showed me that the overall ownership by insiders and institutions was lower than before, and that a few shares had been sold recently. Very likely, some of the insiders were taking profits!

Another popular option would have been to sell only *half* of my shares at the 100-percent profit mark, speculating that even higher profits could be made on the remaining half. The advantage of this technique is that, once you have sold the first half of your shares at 100 percent markup, you have effectively eliminated any further risk to the investment. Even if the remaining shares are sold at zero dollars, you have none of your original capital at risk. Any selling price above the cost of the broker commission is pure profit.

On November 15th, a week after placing my sell order, Brass Eagle opened at $8.80, rose to a high of $9.75 - filling my order along the way - and then closed at its low for the day, or $8.78 (see point "B" on Figure 5-6). As you can see by the chart, as of June 13, 2003, this stock had yet to break through its previous resistance, or to even exceed $9.75, so there is *still* an upside potential. I don't feel too bad, of course. My pre-tax net investment on Brass Eagle was as follows:

BRASS EAGLE (XTRM)	
Sold 200 Shares at $9.25	$1,850.00
Less selling commission & SEC Fee	(10.05)
Bought 200 Shares at $4.50	(900.00)
Less buying commission	(9.99)
NET PROFIT:	**$ 929.96**
7-month Return on Investment:	**102.2%**

FIGURE 5-7. Net return on XTRM, from 4/4/02 through 11/15/02.

Examples of Past Trades

I bought Alaris Medical (AMI) on June 20, 2001 at $1.50 (A) and sold it on December 7th at $3.99 (B), for a net return (after commissions) of 160.2 percent (Figure 5-8). In hindsight, of course, I could have bought it cheaper by buying earlier. In reality, I wanted to wait until insider/institutional ownership had exceeded 80 percent, further "ensuring" a near-term profit. As it turned out, the point at which they held 80 percent of the stock, the price broke through its resistance - a perfect "validation" of the trade. AMI has since risen to exceed $13.00, proving that I was indeed "premature" in selling. But that's just "woulda, shoulda, coulda" thinking. I'm very happy with a 160 percent profit!

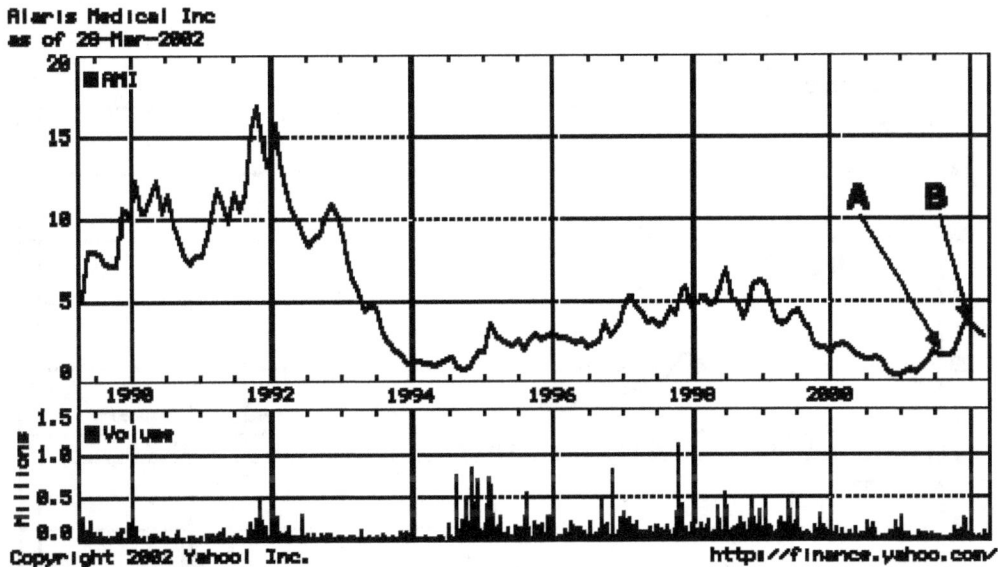

Figure 5-8. AMI - 160.2% Net Return. [Reproduced with permission of Yahoo! Inc. © 2003 by Yahoo! Inc. YAHOO! and the YAHOO! logo are trademarks of Yahoo! Inc.]

I bought Benton Oil (BNO) on September 6, 2001 at $1.55 (A) and sold it on March 6, 2002 at $3.19 (B), for a net return of 100.6 percent (Figure 5-9). With all the oil turmoil and the war against terrorism, this stock could indeed have continued rising, and did for a while. I took the "conservative" route by locking in a mere 100 percent!

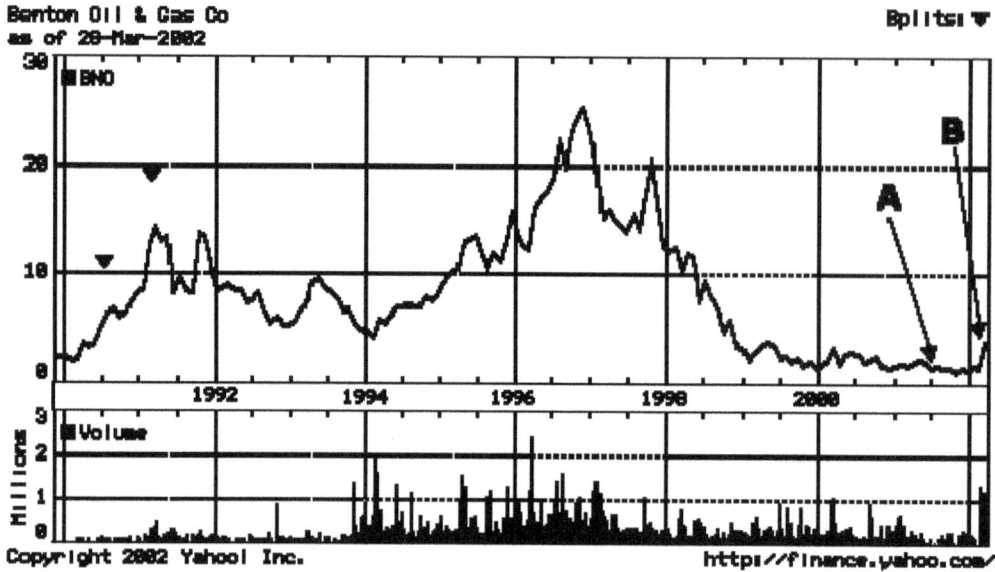

Figure 5-9. BNO - 100.6% Net Return. [Reproduced with permission of Yahoo! Inc. © 2003 by Yahoo! Inc. YAHOO! and the YAHOO! logo are trademarks of Yahoo! Inc.]

One of my earliest trades (with real money) was "Inprise" (INPR), which later changed its name to Borland Software Corp. (BORL). I started buying on April 5, 1999 (Figure 5-10) in a range of $3 to $4, averaging $3.63 (A). The stock hit $18 or so on December 12, 1999, but by the time I could get my sell-order in on the 13th, it had dropped to $14.69 (B), yielding a 288.45 percent net profit. Unfortunately, I hadn't used a trailing stop to lock in higher returns. Lesson learned! As of this writing, BORL has still not broken through that December '99 high but has remained in a sideways trading range.

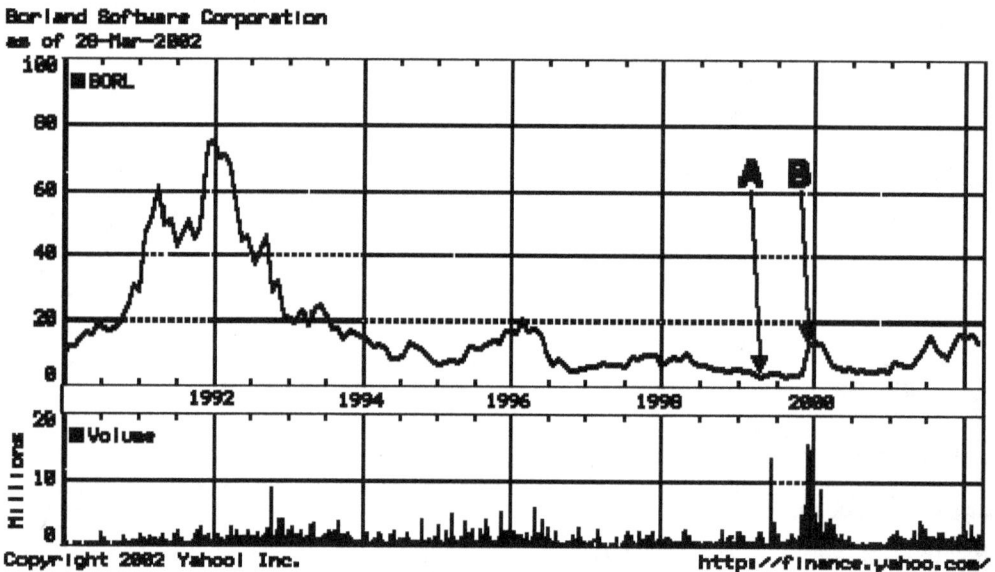

Figure 5-10. INPR/BORL - 288.45% Net Return. [Reproduced with permission of Yahoo! Inc. © 2003 by Yahoo! Inc. YAHOO! and the YAHOO! logo are trademarks of Yahoo! Inc.]

I bought KCS Energy (KCS) on July 25, 2000 at 94-cents (A), and sold half of my shares (Figure 5-11) on September 5th at $2.19 (B). I didn't know whether the rally would continue, of course, but I thought it would since insider/institutional ownership had not diminished, proving they hadn't started "distributing" to the public. I sold the remaining half on January 4, 2001 at

$4.70 for nearly 400 percent returns! Note that the rally continued after a brief dip, doubling again in the June/July 2001 timeframe, and note the steep spike in daily volume during that period - a sure sign of distribution.

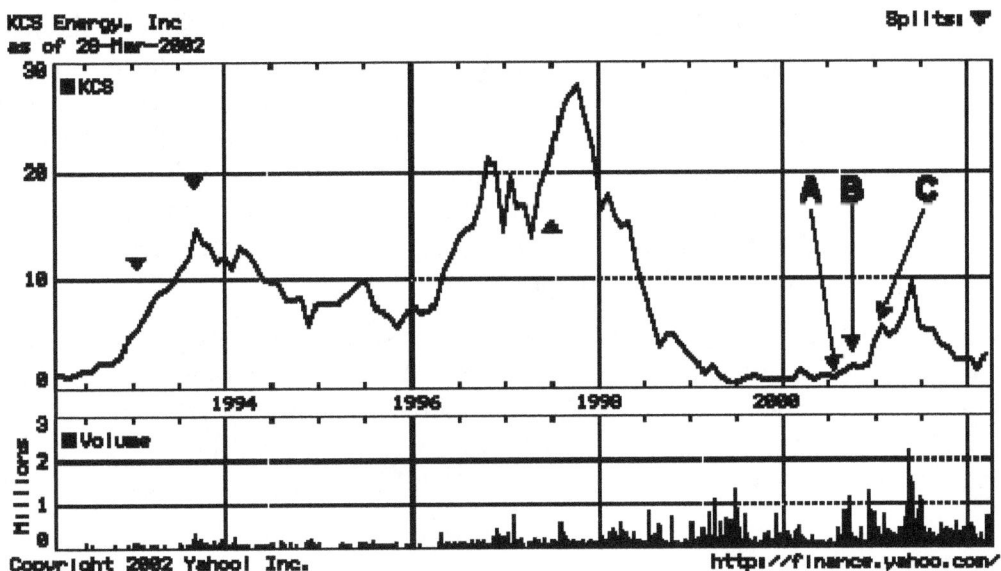

Figure 5-11. KCS - 100.8% and 400% Net Returns. [Reproduced with permission of Yahoo! Inc. © 2003 by Yahoo! Inc. YAHOO! and the YAHOO! logo are trademarks of Yahoo! Inc.]

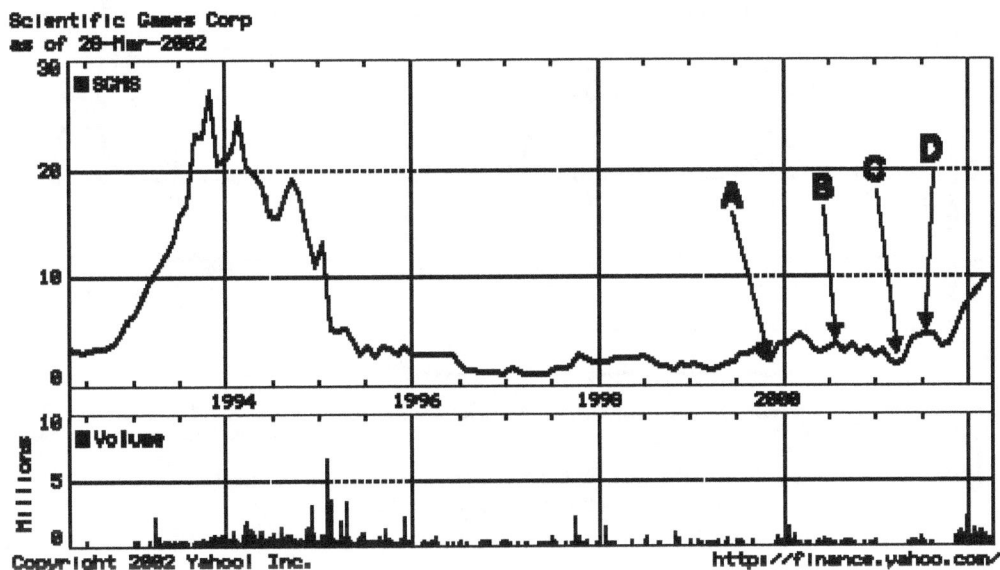

Figure 5-12. SGMS/TTE - 78.1% and 103% Net Returns. [Reproduced with permission of Yahoo! Inc. © 2003 by Yahoo! Inc. YAHOO! and the YAHOO! logo are trademarks of Yahoo! Inc.]

I made a mess of Scientific Games (SGMS), formerly Autotote Corp (TTE), by entering late, exiting too late, then re-entering, and finally exiting too early (Figure 5-12). I'm not complaining, though! I started buying TTE on September 24, 1999 (A), averaging $2.60 per share. I sold out on June 16, 2000 at $4.88 (B), netting 78.1 percent returns. Seeing insider ownership increase rather than decrease, I bought back in on a dip on March 29, 2001 at $1.95 (C), selling just two months later on May 21st at $4.00 (D) for 103 percent net returns. Note where this stock has gone since I left it - I know that other, more aggressive, *Mercenaries* held on to SGMS and waited until the chart trend-line was broken after hitting $10 in April 2002. Again, note the surge in daily volume as the price approached $10, proving that the insiders were indeed dumping their stock.

World Acceptance Corp. (WRLD) is another "classic" story, experiencing insider manipulation back in the mid-1990s, then, going sideways for four years while the insiders re-accumulated the shares (Figure 5-13). By June 28, 2000, over 90 percent of the shares were in their hands, and I bought in at $5.00 (A). I was actually surprised that there were still people willing to sell me any shares, but that's one of the deceptions. If a stock still hasn't moved after four years wouldn't *you* get discouraged and dump it? I had to wait a little less than a year, selling on May 24, 2001 at $8.25 (B) for a net return of 58.65 percent. Obviously, this wasn't as good a return as others I've demonstrated, but how many other investment methods do you know that can reap 58-percent profits in eleven months?

The most interesting part of this story, however, is that my returns were a drop in the bucket, because the "rally" I was riding turned out to be just a minor one. During that time, very few of the institutional owners sold their shares. After peaking at $10 in July 2001, the price retreated and went sideways for almost two years. Then, in May 2003, WRLD broke through $10 again, and has been on a steep rise ever since, hitting $15.99 in June 2003. Does this method pick winners?

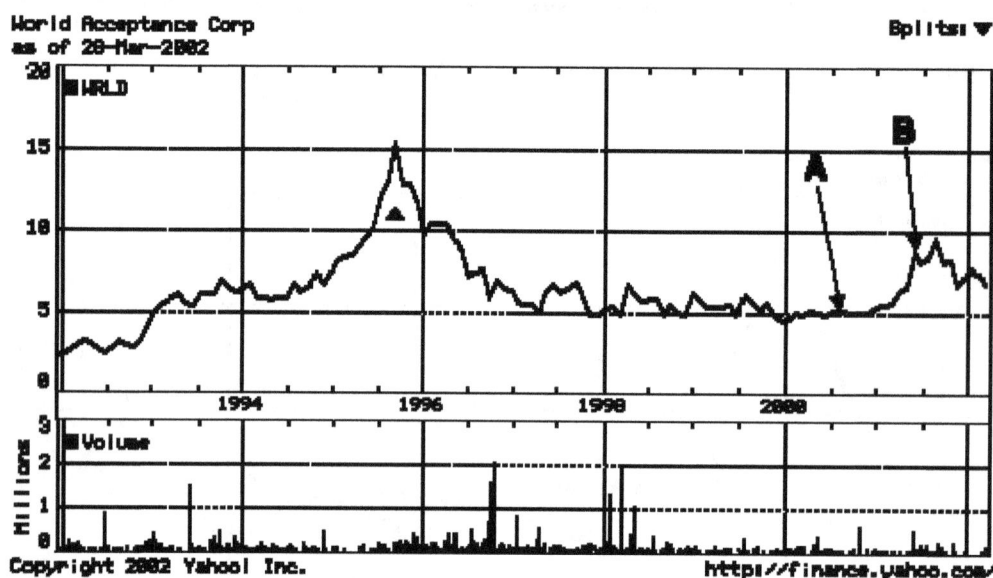

Figure 5-13. WRLD - 58.65% Net Returns. [Reproduced with permission of Yahoo! Inc. © 2003 by Yahoo! Inc. YAHOO! and the YAHOO! logo are trademarks of Yahoo! Inc.]

Portfolio and Money Management

No trading method is complete without a money management plan. Unfortunately, many investment authors barely touch the subject. A *Stock Market Mercenary* must be able to manage everything: finding opportunities, pricing and timing trades, reinvesting profits, managing risk, diversifying the portfolio and planning for the end of the tax year, as if running any business. It is not enough to simply make a 100-percent profit on a trade. That profit must be "exercised" to its maximum capacity, within the limits of your financial goals, to squeeze the most future gain from, and to limit the effects of taxes and inflation on, its use. What follows are suggested guidelines to help you manage your portfolio.

Set Your Risk-Reward Goals

First and foremost, admit to being either a "conservative" or "aggressive" investor. These are not political ideologies, but attitudes that determine how you are likely to trade. A conservative investor is content with less potential profit per year in return for a lower risk of loss. An aggressive investor wants the most possible profit in the least amount of time, and is willing to accept the inevitable higher risk of loss. If you're a senior on a fixed income, with a small nest egg to invest, then you should be the most conservative. If you're in your twenties, you can better afford to rebuild your portfolio in case of a market catastrophe, and can, therefore, be more aggressive. If you are in the middle someplace, you will have to think about your "attitude" a bit more.

In any case, remember the lessons learned in Chapter 2 - capital gains taxes and inflation will consume roughly twelve percent (12%) of your capital each year. Some years, inflation will be more, some years, less. But, the twelve-percent figure is a good average to keep in mind. To overcome this obstacle, it is unlikely that investing in mutual funds will preserve your wealth. Bonds and T-Bills will likewise return less than you need to counter the erosion of capital. The use of tax-free retirement accounts can reduce some of the pressure, but even they are not immune to inflation.

Once you have defined your investing attitude, you should divide your overall portfolio into (at least) three risk categories and calculate the following percentages:

1. **Percentage of capital seeking high returns with higher risk;**

2. **Percentage of capital seeking moderate returns with little risk; and**

3. **Percentage of capital seeking low returns - or a hedge against inflation - with low or "no" risk.**

For this "big picture" plan, you should decide what percentage of your overall capital should be risked in each category. For example, if you are the aggressive type, you may want to have 30 or 40 percent in high-return investments, 60 to 70 percent going after moderate returns, and the balance (zero to 10 percent) in highly secured investments. If you are conservative, you might want only 10 percent of your capital (or none at all) in high-risk ventures, and 40 to 50 percent dedicated to the lowest-risk investments, with the balance seeking moderate returns.

I have already divulged my personal "conservative" leanings, although I find myself somewhere between the two above examples. I tend to risk 20 to 25 percent in high-return strategies, such as the Index Fund method revealed in Chapter 6. I have classified my version of the *Investolator* method for picking individual stocks as "moderate," although it has the potential to earn over 65 percent each year. I like to have between 50 and 70 percent of my capital devoted to this category. You could include Real Estate and most mutual funds in the "moderate" camp as well, however, many mutual funds have shown substantial losses since early-2000.

Finally, my favorite hedge against inflation, and one of the lowest-risk investments I have found, is gold; specifically, American Double Eagles and similar coins. No matter what happens to the economy, gold is gold: it retains its purchasing power. If the bottom were to suddenly drop out from under our economy, I could always barter my gold coins for the necessities of life -

something I could not do with stock certificates! Generally, I like to keep ten percent of my overall portfolio in gold, increasing that percentage during times of geopolitical strife, and lowering it a bit during peacetime. If gold doesn't "glitter" for you, you could substitute cash for gold, or maintain funds in a money market account. Just be aware, however, that inflation will attack your cash wherever you've hidden it.

The decision, of course, is yours, but the key is actually making that decision and sticking to it. Once you've written down your "big picture" plan, be faithful to it for twelve months, and then adjust your percentages if necessary.

The second guideline is: decide the amount of capital you can afford to cheerfully lose in the stock market. Even with a method that naturally minimizes risks by picking stocks at historical bottoms, some risk still remains. How closely you actually follow the method will also determine your ultimate risk.

If you are new to the stock market, you should consider a minimum of $5,000 to get started. This gives you enough capital to make a reasonable profit during your first year. If you can afford to start with more, you will see tangible results even sooner. The biggest mistake that many traders make is undercapitalizing their venture. They are forced to make tiny orders, and their capital gets eaten alive by broker commissions.

Your stock market plan must also be diversified. How many different stocks should you own at any given time? The answer may depend on the amount of starting capital you've chosen. If you have just $5,000 to trade, you might consider the "15 Percent Rule": invest no more than 15 percent of your total portfolio value in any single stock, and always leave 15 percent un-risked in the account. As your account grows (and it will), that 15 percent trade will also grow. Once your account exceeds $10,000, you might consider a "10 Percent Rule" instead, spreading your risk among even more stock investments. As the account grows further, you might consider spreading your investments across multiple strategies, adding more diversity and varying levels of risk to the mix.

Trade Management

The general rule with this *modified* Ted Warren method - which cannot be said with other strategies - is that, unless you have no choice, you shouldn't sell a stock at a loss. Why? You are already buying the stock at low-risk/low-price levels, and should be in no hurry to sell while the manipulators are accumulating. Selling is exactly what they want you to do! If there is something financially wrong with the company you are planning to purchase, you should be able to spot it, by following the steps I have suggested, *before* you make the trade.

This doesn't mean that you will *never* have to take a loss on a stock purchase. Since I began trading this method with real money, I have twice been forced to sell at a loss. In one early case, I bought a stock at the "true" bottom. I hadn't checked the "truth ratio" information that would have told me the company was being liquidated. Oops. Fortunately, there were some *Greater Fools* out there who bought my stock, netting me a 12-percent loss.

More recently, I got caught holding K-Mart stock, purchased for pennies a share, but then suspended when the company announced their Chapter 11 plan to cancel the stock in favor of a whole new "K-Mart" owned entirely by the company's creditors. Within a couple days of that announcement (which left thousands of shareholders holding the bag), most online brokers halted trading, even though the stock continued to trade at the exchanges. I was locked out of selling my stock at *any* price, and the broker offered no explanation as to why they halted trading prematurely. Of course, this is further evidence that brokers are in on the stock manipulation game. In this case, however, I lost all of my K-Mart investment. Had the company made its announcement public, early in the Chapter 11 process, I could have reacted in time to preserve my capital. Needless to say, K-Mart will likely lose thousands of customers from among these "former shareholders." Can you say, "Wal-Mart?"

Some *Mercenaries* are willing to set loss limits on their trades, as they would with other methods that don't recommend buying at the historical bottom. If you are more conservative, this might seem like a good approach. For example, you may have $500 invested in a stock that is headed "south" for some reason. If you are conservative, you might decide that a 10 to 12 percent loss is all the pain you can handle, thus you would sell when your investment sinks to $450 or lower. More aggressive types might set their limit to 25 or even 50 percent. In my experience, when a stock is at the bottom, and the manipulators are doing their best to grab any remaining shares from the public, they will often allow the price to drop below the "bottom" for a short period to completely discourage the market. It's a trick! If you have a hard-and-fast loss limit rule, you run the risk of being "grabbed" yourself. This is why I prefer to not sell a stock unless forced to do so. It works for me, but may not work for you.

Some traders like to buy on the dips in price, thus "averaging down" their cost-per-share over time. If a stock dropped below his initial purchase price, Ted Warren rarely "averaged down" by buying more and more shares at lower prices. But, to many people (including me), this is a logical way to improve one's future profit potential, especially if you're not buying huge blocks of shares. Warren, on the other hand, bought large quantities of stock (in small daily doses, like the insiders, to prevent the public from smelling a rally too soon), and did not want to set new, lower points of "support" - he simply did not wish to *help* the prices stabilize at lower levels. If the market came back to his original price, or even slightly above, he would buy additional shares to "strengthen" the support at his price level.

Personally, I have done it both ways: "averaging down" some stocks, and holding "pat" on others. Since I don't buy in quantities anywhere near Warren's trades, it is doubtful that my trades have influenced the pricing.

Trade management also covers the *type* of stock orders you make. As I stated earlier, I prefer to use "limit orders" for my trades, guaranteeing the price I want at the risk of not being filled at all. Nowadays, "market orders" are too risky. Why? Visit some of the electronic trading venues, and you'll see open orders to buy stocks at one-penny apiece, even though the regular price is $4 or $10 or $50 per share. You will also see sell orders at double or triple the current stock price. This is a trap designed to catch the unwary asleep at the market-order switch. Protect yourself: *use limit orders exclusively in your trades.*

Finally, some traders like to buy stocks "on margin," by borrowing from their broker to buy stocks and then paying interest on those borrowed funds until the stocks are sold. Basically, if the risks are low enough on our historically-low purchase prices to warrant margin-enabled trades, then the advantages may outweigh the risks. Margin orders can virtually double the number of shares you can "afford" – as long as you can afford the interest! I have no particular opinion on the subject, unless you are new to stock trading and have limited funds. In that case, I recommend that you not borrow funds to trade until you have mastered the stock-picking and trade-timing methods covered in this chapter. *If you don't have 100-percent confidence in the outcome of your trades, you shouldn't be risking both capital and interest on an "experiment."*

Dealing With Brokers

I strongly recommend using an online brokerage firm to make your stock trades. For one, you will be making *Contrarian* trades, which a live broker will question every time. Live brokers want to "help" you make your stock-picking and timing decisions. However, this method needs no such input. Besides, using a live broker usually costs more than the commissions charged for unassisted online trades.

Make sure your broker allows trading of OTC (over the counter) stocks as well as stocks listed in the major exchanges, *for the same price*. Also, look for brokers that do not charge a stock-quantity premium. For example, the broker I use currently charges a flat $10.99 for *any* quantity of a particular stock purchased within the same trading day. Thus, if I place an order for 25,000 shares of "XYZ" and they are able to fill only 20,000 shares today, and the remaining 5,000 shares tomorrow, I would pay two commissions ($22). If, however, they fill all 25,000 today, I pay only $11. Further, pick a broker that allows "extended hours" trading for NASDAQ stocks, which trade electronically from 8:00 AM through 8:00 PM Eastern, even though the regular market hours are 9:30 AM through 4:00 PM.

Paper Trading

Before I committed a single penny of real money to my first stock trade, I had already paper-traded Ted Warren's method for 18 months. This resulted in a better education on the strategy than Warren's book alone could possibly deliver. I also had the benefit of all the statistical analysis efforts invested by my team at *Larkin*. We reasoned that, **if one cannot make a profit on paper, risking real money will not magically change the outcome.**

Our paper trading was divided into two portfolios: the original *Investolator* method executed exactly as written, and the method executed with the modifications suggested in this chapter. In most cases, the stocks chosen by both portfolios were the same. However, the modified portfolio earned between 10 and 15 percent more in profits by allowing us to buy at lower prices, or to skip riskier stocks altogether. After that 18-month paper trial, we committed real money to the process, and achieved similar (now-predictable) results, averaging over 70 percent net returns every year since. I believe that this experience alone is reason enough for you to paper-trade the method before risking your hard-earned capital. Although your personal results may be different, they may be much worse if you don't *prove* the method on paper first.

Summary

The first weapon in your *Stock Market Mercenary* arsenal is now at your disposal. But like a real weapon, knowing how to use it in theory is not sufficient. You must now visit the firing range and become a marksman.

As you have seen, the modified *Investolator* method and process are reasonably simple, and the risk is within most people's comfort zone. You are free to employ my modifications or ignore them. The bottom line is: **This method is the antidote to the ailment of mob psychology, and its profit potential is equal to that enjoyed by the very manipulators it exposes.** To borrow an old Chrysler slogan, "If you can find a better strategy, *buy it*."

Chapter 6: Leveraged Diversification

Multiply your Index Fund returns into huge profits

Financial advisors the world over tell us that, building a diversified portfolio lowers our overall risk by spreading that risk over many stock investments. When most people hear the word "diversification," however, they immediately think, "mutual fund." Granted, a mutual fund is in the business of selecting a large group of stocks meeting a specific set of criteria. So, because there are many different stocks in the fund, it must, therefore, be a low-risk investment. Right? Not necessarily. The *majority* of stocks held by a mutual fund are those that meet the rules of the fund manager's strategy - which can often be very limiting. Thus, if economic forces negatively affect stocks within the fund's narrow parameters, then the gains of the *entire fund* are in jeopardy. In order to be truly "diversified," a fund must have many exceptions to the rule that smooth out the short-term ups and downs of the market.

Further, mutual funds are risky simply because they have had a lousy overall track record, especially during bear markets. Even the best fund managers cannot show a profit every year, and very few of them can match the annual performance of the S&P 500 index. Exceptions include the few mutual funds that specialize in surviving bear markets. For example, the "Prudent Bear Fund" has outperformed the market since the Tech Bubble burst in 2000. How? Approximately two-thirds of the fund's 2002 holdings were "short" the market, benefiting from the downtrend. Of course, during a sustained *bull* market, such a fund would be expected to under-perform the indexes. Despite some rare exceptions, *generally the most consistent and profitable mutual funds cannot overcome the long-term combined erosion of capital gains taxes and inflation.*

"Owning" an Index

Many of the exchanges, spurred by countless requests from public investors, have in recent years introduced ETFs (exchange-traded funds) and other instruments, allowing traders to "own" a piece of the major stock indexes. For example, a share in the "Diamond" (DIA) fund represents a unit of ownership in all thirty of the Dow Jones[SM] Industrial Average companies. Likewise, a "Spider" (SPDR or SPY) represents a unit of ownership in the SPDR trust, which is like owning a piece of all 500 companies in the Standard and Poor's 500 index. The tech-heavy NASDAQ 100 index can be "owned" with shares in the "QQQ" fund.

ETFs can also represent individual sectors of the market, like transportation stocks, or computer networking stocks, and so forth. As of this writing, there are over 100 ETFs available, representing billions of Dollars in assets.

Another fund instrument, called "iShares," was introduced within the past four years, and has grown to track nearly 80 different indexes. For example, although a full-valued share of the Dow Jones[SM] Industrial Average might cost you $9,300 today, the "IYJ" iShare, that mirrors the Dow, costs roughly $42.25, a 1-to-220 ratio. Likewise, the "IYY" iShare represents the "Dow Jones Total Market Index Fund," owning stock in over 1,570 companies. As of mid-June 2003, assets in the "IYY" exceeded $220 million.[91]

Like individual stocks, iShares and other ETF equities each have stock symbols and are traded just like public corporation shares. But the key advantage is that they track the gains and losses of their respective indexes on a nearly one-to-one basis, thus offering a "diversified" investment at a fraction of the cost. For example, if the S&P 500 is your index of choice, you can buy "Spiders" and benefit as if you owned a share of every company in the index. Thus, if you bought 100 SPDR shares on the first trading day of January, and sold on the last trading day of December, you would have gained or lost the same percentage of your investment as was realized by the overall S&P 500 index.

Figure 6-1 illustrates the relative performance of four major index funds. Note that, except during the Tech-Bubble period (1999-2001), the Dow Jones[SM] Industrial Average has outperformed the other indexes in most years. Since we have already stated that index fund performance often exceeds that of mutual funds, and since most index funds represent a larger and far more "diversified" collection of stocks than mutual funds, it follows that buying ETFs is a low-risk proposition. Right? Not necessarily! *Lower* risk, maybe; *low* risk, unlikely.

As much as any other investment vehicle, index funds can be affected by geopolitical events, global oil price fluctuations, wars, United Nations actions (or inactions), trade embargos, treaties, and acts of terrorism. However, the broadest index funds are less-subject to *some* risks, including those caused by the manipulation of individual stocks. Only in cases where many of the largest public companies are being manipulated simultaneously will index funds, containing the manipulated stocks, be affected - as occurred during the Tech Bubble. Further, index funds are not subject to the narrow stock-selection parameters employed by mutual fund managers, but generally include all stocks larger than a certain minimum size, or all stocks within a particular business sector, regardless of their fundamentals.

Earlier I stated that the advantage of ETF stocks was that they track the indexes on a one-to-one basis. Unfortunately, that is also their *disadvantage*. If the S&P 500 rises 12 percent in one year, and you've been holding some Spiders for purposes of diversification, you will also post gains of 12 percent. Of course, your original capital will be eroded by inflation, as will your 12-percent gain, and you will have to pay capital gains tax on the profits. Based upon the average historical inflation in this country, you will have gained little.

---

[91] Source: www.iShares.com

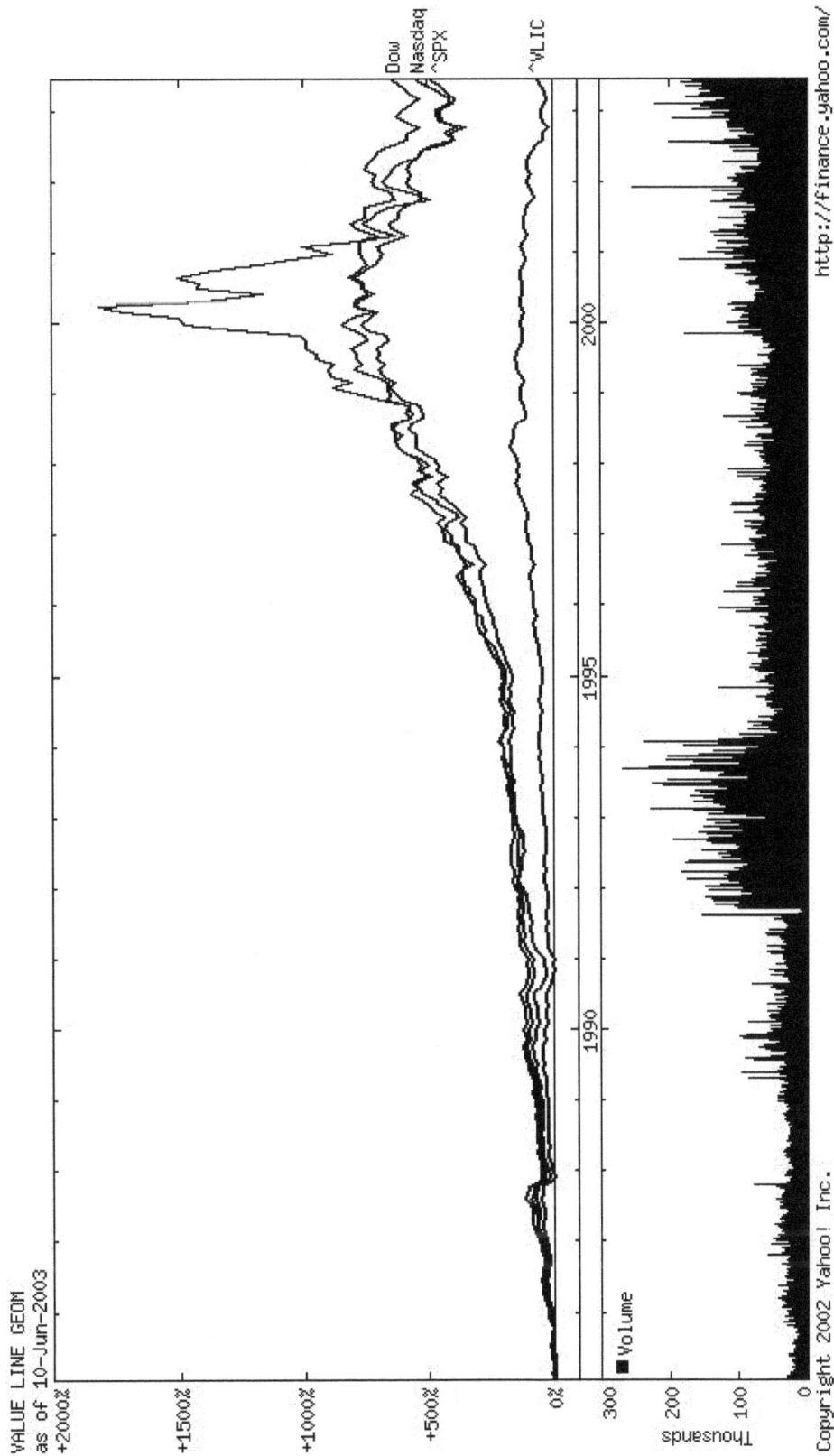

FIGURE 6-1. Relative performance of four major indexes since 1985, Dow Jones^{SM} Industrial Average, NASDAQ, S&P 500 and Value Line. Note the volatility of the NASDAQ, especially during the Tech Bubble (1999-2001).

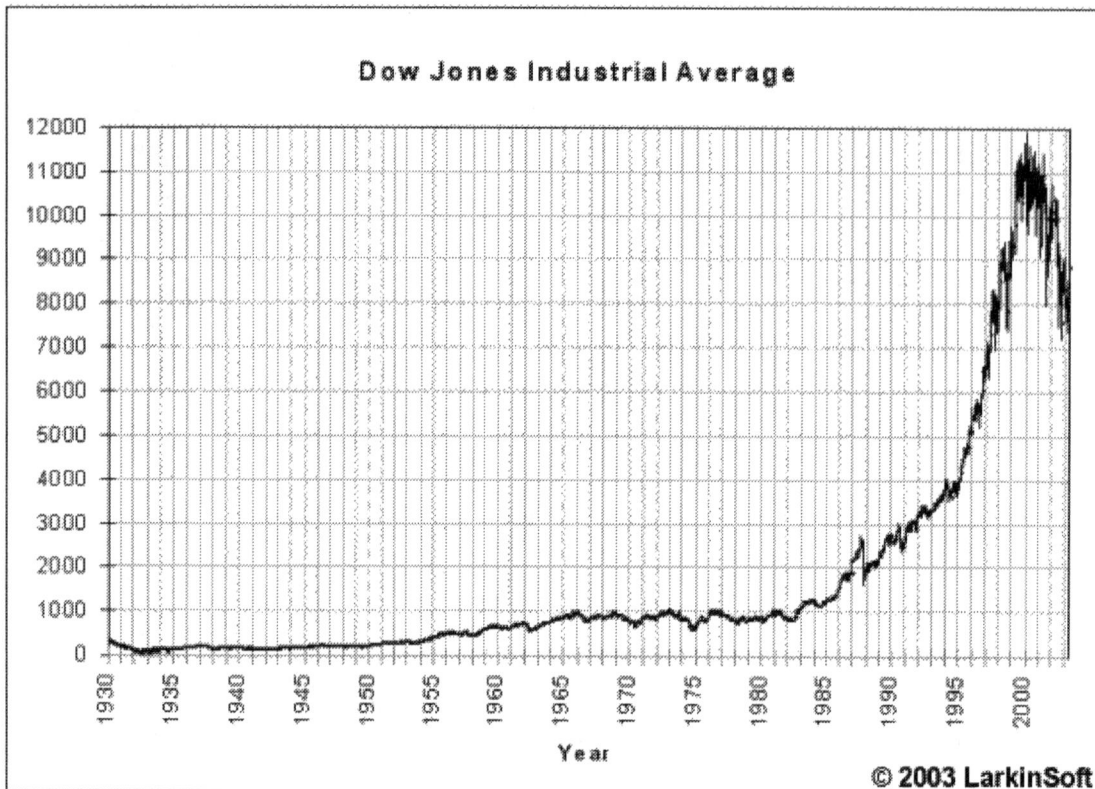

FIGURE 6-2. Dow Jones^{SM} Industrial Average from January 1930 through May 2003. [Reproduced with permission of Larkin Industries, Inc. © 2003 by LarkinSoft. LarkinSoft is a trademark of Larkin Industries, Inc.]

From late-1932 through early-2000, the U.S. has experienced a generally bullish market, as illustrated by the Dow Jones^{SM} Industrial Average chart in Figure 6-2. Since the bursting of the Tech Bubble in March 2000, however, the market has been correcting itself sharply, and the major stock indexes have not fared as well since that date, except for short-term bull rallies within the overall downtrend. Therefore, unless the market is experiencing a brief bull rally, the only real advantage to ETF investments is diversification - or, slightly lowered risk.

That is, unless you know how to use *leverage*.

Leverage Is Power

A great example of the power of leverage regularly occurs in Real Estate. Say you are buying a $200,000 home. Instead of paying the full price in cash, you might make a small down payment and finance the balance with a mortgage. Assuming your down payment is 20 percent, or $40,000, your "risk" is presently limited to that amount. After twelve months, however, the home may have appreciated by five percent, or $10,000. Ignoring any pay-down of your mortgage during that year, what is the return on your investment? Five percent? No, *twenty-five* percent - you "deposited" $40,000 and gained $10,000 within a year.

Leverage is how some of the greatest fortunes in history were made. And many of today's most successful market investors use the power of Futures and Options in the commodities market to leverage their capital.

Most people shudder when the topic of investing in commodities comes up. Everyone seems to know someone who "lost it all" in pork bellies or precious metals. And most people label commodities investing as an extremely high-risk proposition. Under normal circumstances, I would have to agree. The commodities market can indeed be riskier than the stock market, and it is also subject to manipulation - just like the stock market.

The one redeeming quality of investing in commodity futures, however, is the ability to leverage your capital, *potentially earning five- or ten-times the profits on the same amount of risked capital*. *Stock Market Mercenaries* usually perk up when they hear about multiplying their profits by five or ten times. (I'll wait...)

If you're not familiar with the mechanics of leverage in commodities, let me briefly explain.[92] A futures contract is merely a promise to buy or sell a certain quantity of a product by a future date at a certain price. For example, wheat farmers will promise to *sell* their crops by the end of their harvest season, and will thus "sell" futures contracts, representing a particular crop date, at a market price. One wheat futures contract controls 5,000 bushels, and is priced anywhere from 300 to 400 cents per bushel. Meanwhile, flourmills will promise to buy the wheat at a price, and will thus "buy" wheat futures contracts. What's interesting is that neither the buyers nor the sellers actually pay the full value of those contracts at the time they place their orders. All they do is make a good faith, refundable "margin" deposit, often a mere fraction (3 to 10 percent) of the face value. Of course, the players I've described actually do buy or sell the wheat. When the due-date arrives to fulfill the contracts, the wheat is physically delivered and the contract price is settled in full.

In the meantime, speculators, believing that wheat prices may go up or down, are also buying and selling wheat futures in the market; except, they have no intention of actually buying or supplying wheat. They are simply trying to *leverage* their margin deposits into large profits. For example, if today's wheat price is 340-cents (per bushel), and they can control a 5,000-bushel contract worth $17,000 with a $1,148 deposit, this results in nearly 15-to-1 leverage. If the price moves up just 20 cents, to $3.60 per bushel, the speculator earns $1,000 in profit when he sells his contract to another speculator, **and** he gets his $1,148 deposit back. That's an 87-percent return on capital he never actually surrendered. Of course, if the price goes the other way, the speculator would now *owe* $1,000, but would still get his deposit back upon liquidation.

If you want a crash course in how commodities are actually traded at the exchanges, drop by your local video store and rent the comedy, "Trading Places," starring Dan Aykroyd and Eddie Murphy. The last 20 minutes of the movie is an entertaining primer on the subject. The movie also illustrates how large brokerages can manipulate the frozen concentrated orange juice market!

---

[92] There are dozens of publications and websites available on the mechanics of commodities investing. Most online commodities brokers also offer tutorials and "simulated trading" services, allowing you to practice (and prove) your methods before committing real money.

The Seasonal Forces

The difference between winners and losers in the commodities market often boils down to three principles: leverage, money management, and a keen understanding of seasonal price patterns. The leverage part should now be obvious. Sound money management in this arena requires using "stop loss" orders to limit losses if the market goes against you; and always having twice the capital in your investment account than you ever have at-risk in contracts. Seasonal price patterns are a natural result of supply and demand, tied to harvest times for agricultural products, slaughter times for meat animals, times when global banks settle their accounts, and times when governments settle their debts and fiscal budgets. These patterns are not "sure things" every year, of course, but they do provide confirmation of *general trends* that tend to repeat in most years.

For example, December wheat contract prices tend to rise in October, while December corn rarely does. Pork bellies (where our morning bacon comes from) often rally in both August and late-October. Sugar usually tops out in the June-July timeframe, falling sharply through September, then heading back up during the fall. Cocoa tends to hit bottom in the summer and rally big in the fall and early winter (apparently, people really do drink more hot cocoa when it's cold). Finally, the United States government settles most of its accounts near the end of its fiscal year, which ends on September 30th. Dating back to the early 1800s, October has been the perennial "correction" period, most likely due to money supply and government gold reserve adjustments.

More recently, October has become the "shakeout" month for the stock market. Theories abound on why this happens. For example, October is the month in which most corporate third-quarter earnings reports are made public. Companies begin "confessing" and "guiding" their poor end-of-summer results in mid-September, which usually sparks the downward slide in their stock prices.

Another theory is that institutional traders (mutual fund managers, banks and insurance companies, etc.) clean out their portfolios of under-performing stocks near the end of each month, but especially in October. Of course, if a lot of companies are "confessing" poor earnings, it makes sense that fund managers would want to protect their portfolios. Since mutual funds compete for ratings, they would be naturally motivated to improve their performance numbers after a rough summer. So, these under-performing shares are dumped in large volumes, late in October, which puts even more downward pressure on those stocks, thus, affecting the overall market.

Yet another theory about the "magic" of October was suggested to me by a colleague, presently under contract with a large accounting agency within the federal government. He believes that the inner-workings of the government budgetary cycle may have something to do with this phenomenon. I quote him here under conditions of anonymity:

> If an agency has overspent its budget prior to September, there is nothing left for the government contractors until late-October or early-November when funds begin to flow again. Since many of the contractors are public corporations, it makes sense that their stock values would drop a little after a third quarter with reduced government revenues.[93]

---

[93] Source: Consultant for the federal government, specializing in budget accounting. Name withheld.

Since only a fraction of public corporations generate revenues from government contracts, however, I would suggest that the annual October slump is likely caused by a combination of *all* these theories. **Whether or not these *theories* are true, is irrelevant. A recurring seasonal pattern in the overall stock market exists.**

If you look at the major "corrections" of 1929, 1987, and 2000 through 2002, you will find the bottoms for each year in the mid-September to late-October period. For example, in 1987, the low for the Dow occurred on October 20th at 1,616.20. In 2000, the Dow hit bottom on October 18th at 9,571.40. In the following two years, the lows were posted on September 21st (7,926.90) and October 10th (7,181.47), respectively. The terrorist attack on 11-Sep-2001 appears to have accelerated the cycle that year.

Using monthly charts of the Dow, covering the past 23 years, I have identified the recurring up-trends that illustrate part of the annual "stock market cycle." Note that each trend line begins in the September-October period and is - with rare exception - "broken" in the spring or early summer, falling back to a lower level thereafter. Of course, the Dow represents only 30 industrial companies, but, because they are the largest, they tend to reflect the overall direction of the stock market.

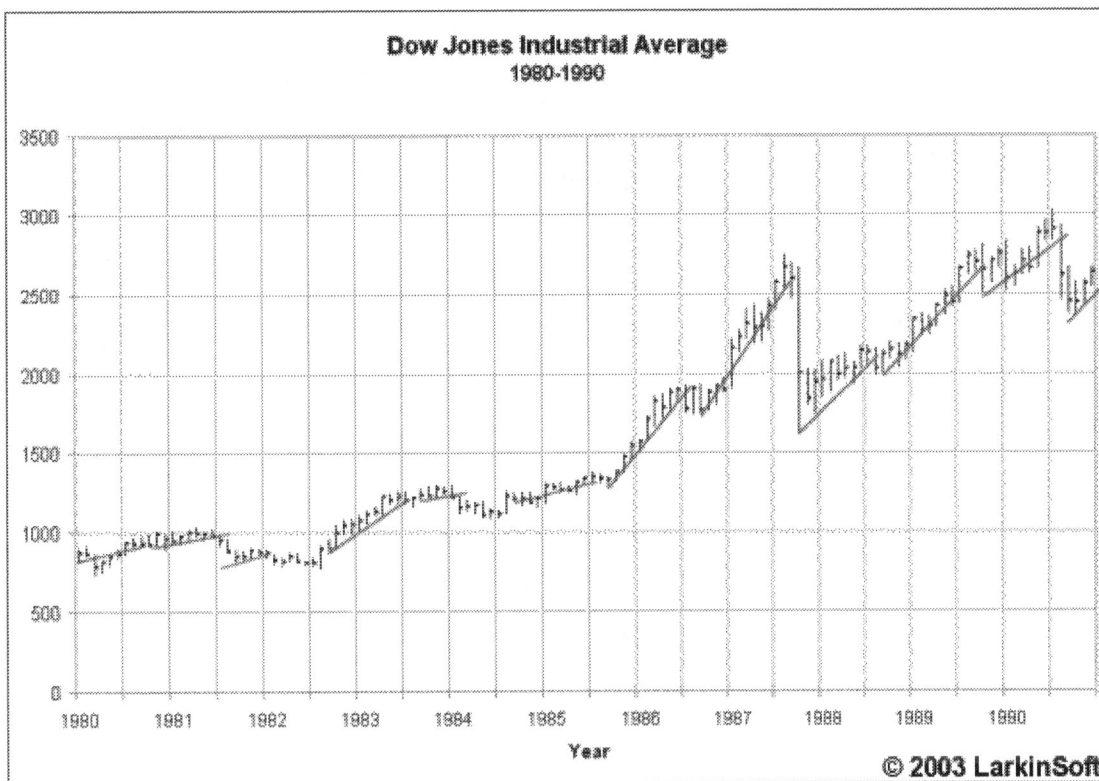

FIGURE 6-3. Dow Jones[SM] recurring trends, 1980 to 1990. Each tick represents the monthly high and low, as well as the closing price for the month. [Reproduced with permission of Larkin Industries, Inc. © 2003 by LarkinSoft. LarkinSoft is a trademark of Larkin Industries, Inc.]

Dow Jones Industrial Average
1990-2000

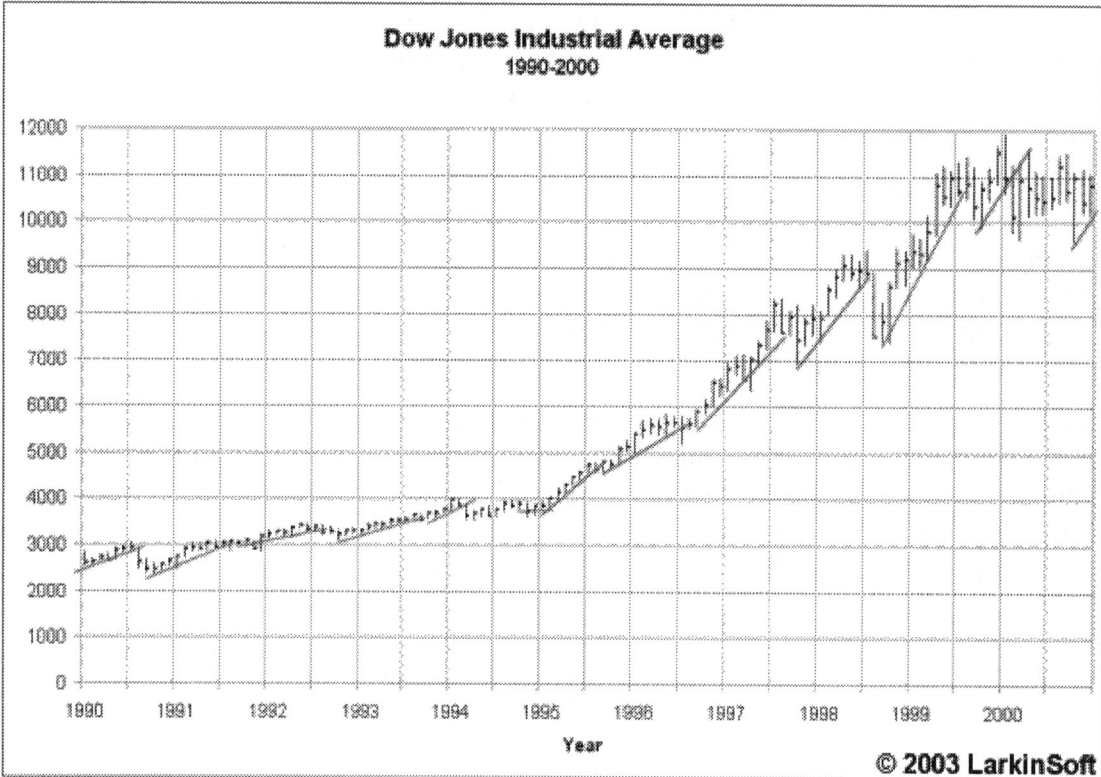

FIGURE 6-4. Dow Jones^{SM} recurring trends, 1990 to 2000. [Reproduced with permission of Larkin Industries, Inc. © 2003 by LarkinSoft. LarkinSoft is a trademark of Larkin Industries, Inc.]

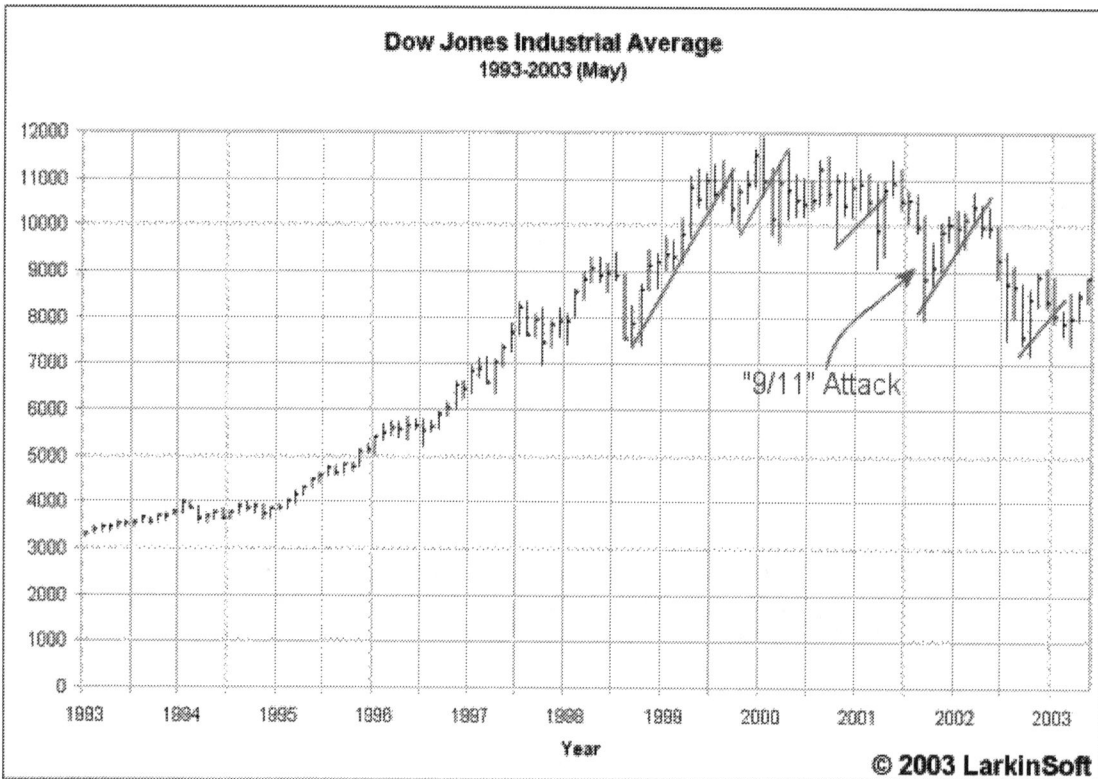

Dow Jones Industrial Average
1993-2003 (May)

"9/11" Attack

© 2003 LarkinSoft

FIGURE 6-5. Dow Jones^{SM} recurring trends, 1993 to 2003. [Reproduced with permission of Larkin Industries, Inc. © 2003 by LarkinSoft. LarkinSoft is a trademark of Larkin Industries, Inc.]

In most years, the late-October lows are not the *annual* lows as well, but they tend to be lower than the heights reached the following spring. Since 1930, the annual lows were posted in September or October only 20 percent of the time. Within the past 20 years, however, seven (35%) annual lows occurred within that two-month period. However, for purposes of the "fiscal cycle" we have identified, **it does not matter that the low for the *year* occurs in September or October - only that the low for that period leads to profitable highs the *following year*.**

Statistically, in fact, you can almost set your watch to the late-October low rising through the following spring and early summer, then "correcting" itself in August or September. This indicates a fiscal cycle in the stock market, lagging one month behind the federal government's fiscal year. These patterns seem to happen whether we are in a long-term bull or bear market. The difference is, during bear markets each October low tends to be lower that the previous year, and during bull markets the October low tends to be higher each year.

Dow Jones Industrial Average Cycle Statistics - 1930 to 1955						
Period	Cycle Low	Low Value	Cycle High	High Value	Net Gain	% Gain
1930-1931	22-Oct-30	181.50	2-Mar-31	191.90	10.40	5.73%
1931-1932	5-Oct-31	85.50	8-Mar-32	89.90	4.40	5.15%
1932-1933	10-Oct-32	57.70	18-Jul-33	110.50	52.80	91.51%
1933-1934	20-Oct-33	83.60	20-Apr-34	107.00	23.40	27.99%
1934-1935	17-Sep-34	85.70	31-Jul-35	127.00	41.30	48.19%
1935-1936	3-Oct-35	127.00	28-Jul-36	168.20	41.20	32.44%
1936-1937	17-Sep-36	164.80	10-Mar-37	195.60	30.80	18.69%
1937-1938	19-Oct-37	115.80	25-Jul-38	146.30	30.50	26.34%
1938-1939	26-Sep-38	127.90	10-Mar-39	152.70	24.80	19.39%
1939-1940	18-Sep-39	147.40	8-Apr-40	152.10	4.70	3.19%
1940-1941	13-Sep-40	127.20	22-Jul-41	131.10	3.90	3.07%
1941-1942	31-Oct-41	117.40	15-Jul-42	109.50	(7.90)	-6.73%
1942-1943	11-Sep-42	105.60	15-Jul-43	146.40	40.80	38.64%
1943-1944	13-Oct-43	135.90	10-Jul-44	150.90	15.00	11.04%
1944-1945	14-Sep-44	142.70	26-Jun-45	169.60	26.90	18.85%
1945-1946	17-Sep-45	173.30	29-May-46	213.40	40.10	23.14%
1946-1947	30-Oct-46	160.50	25-Jul-47	187.70	27.20	16.95%
1947-1948	26-Sep-47	174.40	14-Jun-48	194.50	20.10	11.53%
1948-1949	27-Sep-48	175.80	30-Mar-49	179.20	3.40	1.93%
1949-1950	20-Sep-49	177.60	12-Jun-50	229.20	51.60	29.05%
1950-1951	6-Sep-50	217.40	4-May-51	264.40	47.00	21.62%
1951-1952	29-Oct-51	256.40	31-Jul-52	280.30	23.90	9.32%
1952-1953	23-Oct-52	262.00	18-Mar-53	292.00	30.00	11.45%
1953-1954	15-Sep-53	254.40	30-Jul-54	349.20	94.80	37.26%
1954-1955	10-Sep-54	345.50	26-Jul-55	471.70	126.20	36.53%
1955-1956	11-Oct-55	433.20	9-Apr-56	524.40	91.20	21.05%

FIGURE 6-6. Dow Jones[SM] Industrial Average Cycle Statistics, 1930-1955.

The three tables (above and below) list every fall-to-summer cycle in the Dow Jones[SM] Industrial Average since 1930. The 2003 high on June 6th was the latest available as this book went to press, however I would expect an even higher number by July. In fact, *40 percent* of the cycle highs since 1930 have been posted in July. Within the 74 years recorded in these statistics, only *two* years failed to produce a cycle gain: 1941 to 1942, and 1983 to 1984.

Dow Jones Industrial Average Cycle Statistics - 1956 to 1980						
Period	Cycle Low	Low Value	Cycle High	High Value	Net Gain	% Gain
1956-1957	1-Oct-56	463.80	16-Jul-57	523.10	59.30	12.79%
1957-1958	22-Oct-57	416.20	31-Jul-58	508.40	92.20	22.15%
1958-1959	10-Sep-58	514.60	30-Jul-59	678.70	164.10	31.89%
1959-1960	22-Sep-59	613.30	9-Jun-60	663.60	50.30	8.20%
1960-1961	25-Oct-60	564.20	22-May-61	714.70	150.50	26.67%
1961-1962	25-Sep-61	688.90	16-Mar-62	727.10	38.20	5.55%
1962-1963	24-Oct-62	549.70	5-Jun-63	733.00	183.30	33.35%
1963-1964	30-Sep-63	728.60	20-Jul-64	855.20	126.60	17.38%
1964-1965	10-Sep-64	852.70	14-May-65	944.80	92.10	10.80%
1965-1966	10-Sep-65	911.70	21-Apr-66	961.90	50.20	5.51%
1966-1967	10-Oct-66	735.70	21-Jul-67	918.70	183.00	24.87%
1967-1968	31-Oct-67	876.20	3-May-68	935.70	59.50	6.79%
1968-1969	12-Sep-68	908.10	14-May-69	974.90	66.80	7.36%
1969-1970	9-Oct-69	794.00	25-Mar-70	803.30	9.30	1.17%
1970-1971	22-Sep-70	741.50	28-Apr-71	958.10	216.60	29.21%
1971-1972	28-Oct-71	827.80	30-May-72	979.50	151.70	18.33%
1972-1973	17-Oct-72	917.10	8-Mar-73	985.30	68.20	7.44%
1973-1974	14-Sep-73	873.30	14-Mar-74	904.00	30.70	3.52%
1974-1975	4-Oct-74	573.20	15-Jul-75	888.90	315.70	55.08%
1975-1976	1-Oct-75	780.50	24-Mar-76	1018.00	237.50	30.43%
1976-1977	12-Oct-76	928.30	16-Mar-77	971.60	43.30	4.66%
1977-1978	25-Oct-77	792.80	6-Jun-78	879.30	86.50	10.91%
1978-1979	30-Oct-78	782.10	11-Apr-79	884.60	102.50	13.11%
1979-1980	22-Oct-79	796.00	30-Jul-80	946.90	150.90	18.96%
1980-1981	31-Oct-80	911.60	27-Apr-81	1031.00	119.40	13.10%

FIGURE 6-7. Dow Jones[SM] Industrial Average Cycle Statistics, 1956-1980.
[Reproduced with permission of Larkin Industries, Inc. © 2003 by LarkinSoft. LarkinSoft is a trademark of Larkin Industries, Inc.]

Of course, the gains depicted in these tables assume *perfect* timing on the part of an investor, as well as the clairvoyance necessary to divine the cycle bottom on the day it occurs, within the exchange's trading hours, so that a trade can be placed. Similar talent would be required for the profitable "exit" the following year. The point here is that, using reasonable trend-following techniques, profits can be made from the Dow and other indexes by recognizing the recurring patterns within the general stock market.

During long-term bear markets (such as our present one), the drop from the spring/summer cycle highs, through the following lows in September-October, can also provide an opportunity to profit. For example, in Figure 6-8, the Dow's cycle high of 11436.40 was reached on 21-May-01, later dropping to a low of 7926.90 on 21-Sep-01. Within that four-month period, the Dow lost over 3,500 points, or 30 percent! Had a *Stock Market Mercenary* "shorted" the Dow after taking profits on the previous cycle high (which gained 19.49%), the total 12-month returns could have been nearly 50 percent.

Dow Jones Industrial Average Cycle Statistics - 1981 to 2003 (partial)						
Period	Cycle Low	Low Value	Cycle High	High Value	Net Gain	% Gain
1981-1982	28-Sep-81	807.50	7-May-82	876.50	69.00	8.54%
1982-1983	30-Sep-82	891.30	17-Jun-83	1260.70	369.40	41.45%
1983-1984	16-Sep-83	1210.20	16-Mar-84	1197.20	(13.00)	-1.07%
1984-1985	10-Oct-84	1158.20	23-Jul-85	1372.20	214.00	18.48%
1985-1986	18-Sep-85	1283.70	2-Jul-86	1922.70	639.00	49.78%
1986-1987	29-Sep-86	1733.00	31-Jul-87	2588.30	855.30	49.35%
1987-1988	20-Oct-87	1616.20	6-Jul-88	2169.50	553.30	34.23%
1988-1989	13-Sep-88	2055.30	31-Jul-89	2668.30	613.00	29.83%
1989-1990	16-Oct-89	2496.90	17-Jul-90	3024.30	527.40	21.12%
1990-1991	11-Oct-90	2344.30	3-Jun-91	3057.50	713.20	30.42%
1991-1992	9-Oct-91	2925.50	2-Jun-92	3435.30	509.80	17.43%
1992-1993	5-Oct-92	3087.40	27-Jul-93	3604.90	517.50	16.76%
1993-1994	21-Sep-93	3501.50	18-Mar-94	3911.80	410.30	11.72%
1994-1995	5-Oct-94	3736.20	27-Jul-95	4768.00	1031.80	27.62%
1995-1996	10-Oct-95	4638.40	23-May-96	5833.00	1194.60	25.75%
1996-1997	10-Sep-96	5681.70	31-Jul-97	8329.00	2647.30	46.59%
1997-1998	28-Oct-97	6936.50	17-Jul-98	9412.60	2476.10	35.70%
1998-1999	8-Oct-98	7399.80	19-Jul-99	11321.60	3921.80	53.00%
1999-2000	18-Oct-99	9884.20	12-Apr-00	11600.40	1716.20	17.36%
2000-2001	18-Oct-00	9571.40	21-May-01	11436.40	1865.00	19.49%
2001-2002	21-Sep-01	7926.90	8-Mar-02	10728.90	2802.00	35.35%
2002-2003	10-Oct-02	7181.47	6-Jun-03	9248.71	2067.24	28.79%

FIGURE 6-8. Dow Jones[SM] Industrial Average Cycle Statistics, 1981-2003.
[Reproduced with permission of Larkin Industries, Inc. © 2003 by LarkinSoft. LarkinSoft is a trademark of Larkin Industries, Inc.]

As you can see by the earlier trend chart (Figure 6-5) through 2003, each October low is considerably lower than the previous year's cycle low - confirming the obvious: a bear market. (We do not need economists, or the government, to tell us we are in a bull or bear market. A few seconds looking at a long-term chart tells us what we need to know!)

In the stock market, of course, many investors classify short sellers as "un-American," since such traders appear to be betting *against* prosperity. In the commodities market, however, "selling short" is nearly as common a practice as "buying long." To survive this game, one must do whatever is necessary to make a profit.

So, what does all this have to do with diversifying a stock portfolio?

Let me answer with a qualifying question: *If you could diversify your stock holdings like an Index Fund while leveraging your capital like a Futures Contract, and do it with relative safety, would you consider it a worthwhile investment?*

The Leveraged Index Fund Strategy

Assume for a moment that you have $10,000 designated for higher-return, higher-risk investments. Assume further that you wish to "diversify" this capital by investing in the Dow Jones^{SM} Industrials. You would have four options:

1. You could buy stock in each of the thirty companies that make up the Dow (General Electric, Microsoft, Wal-Mart, Coca-Cola, etc.), taking care to buy shares in the same proportions as they are represented in the Dow. Your returns would loosely mimic the performance of the Dow, but you would have to manage 30 different stocks.

2. You could buy $10,000 worth of "Diamond" shares (DIA) in the Dow Jones^{SM} exchange-traded fund. Your returns would closely mimic the performance of the Dow.

3. You could buy $10,000 worth of iShares in the Dow-simulated (IYJ) fund. Your returns would also closely mimic the Dow's with slightly higher variation.

4. You could open a margin trading account with a discount commodities broker and risk around *half* of your capital in a "Dow Jones Industrial Average Futures $10" (DJ) contract, through the Chicago Board of Trade (CBOT). The points gained and lost would track the Dow closely, but each point would be worth Ten Dollars ($10).

Before I get to the details of that last option, let's find out the potential difference in dollars between the first three options and the fourth. For example, using the table in Figure 6-8, and picking the 2000-2001 cycle, you attempt to buy the Dow in mid-October 2000 at around 9,600 points and sell the following May at a "conservative" 11,000 points. These entry and exit figures assume that you're *late* in detecting the cycle trend - a very common scenario!

Our hypothetical gain is 1,400 points, or 14.58 percent. Assuming you had chosen any of the first three Dow options above, you would have earned roughly $1,458 in gross profit on your $10,000 investment within a seven-month period. Not bad! That's about 25 percent profit, annualized (before commissions).

Under option 4, you instruct your commodities broker to "buy long one June 2001 DJ contract at market," and a margin deposit of $5,400 is allocated from your account. The rest of your money remains available in case you need to cover a margin call (which happens only if you lose more than $1,400 per DJ contract). The DJ futures contract is worth $10 per point, so your gross profit in May is $14,000 on the Dow's 1,400-point rise. Upon selling your contract, your $14,000 profit is added to your account, and your original $5,400 deposit is released back to you, plus any "margin" amounts you may have paid along the way. Your return on investment would be 140 percent on your total capital, or 259 percent against the original portion you risked, for a seven-month trade.

So, the Dow moved 1,400 points, and you had the opportunity to earn either $1,458 or $14,000 for the same movement and capital. **Using the commodities market, your earnings would have been 9.6 times the gains in the stock market.** Now, that's leverage! Yes, your risk was higher - you might have had to cover margins whenever the market dipped too low. But, there are ways to manage your trades to limit these risks, as we will see.

Picking and Timing Trades

If you are new to commodities investing, you may not realize how many stock index funds can actually be traded through commodities exchanges. The table below lists my five favorites, but there are many others, including European and Asian stock indexes.

Popular Index Funds via Commodities Exchanges							
Commodity	Symbol	Exchange	Margin Deposit	Main-tenance	Value / Point	Contract Months	Stocks In Fund
Dow Jones Average $10	DJ	CBOT	$ 5,400	$ 4,000	$ 10.00	Mar, Jun, Sep, Dec	30
Dow Jones Mini Average $5	YM	CBOT	$ 2,700	$ 2,000	$ 5.00	Mar, Jun, Sep, Dec	30
S&P 500 E-Mini	ES	CME	$ 3,563	$ 2,850	$ 50.00	Mar, Jun, Sep, Dec	500*
S&P 500 Index	SP	CME	$17,813	$14,250	$250.00	Mar, Jun, Sep, Dec	500*
Value Line Stock Index	MV	KCBT	$ 4,500	$ 3,600	$100.00	Mar, Jun, Sep, Dec	1650*
							* Quantity varies
CBOT = Chicago Board of Trade | CME = Chicago Mercantile Exchange | KCBT = Kansas City Board of Trade							

FIGURE 6-9. Dan's favorite commodities index funds. Margin and Maintenance amounts are subject to change at any time. The figures above were accurate as of June-2003.

Of the major index funds available, the Kansas City Board of Trade's "Value Line Stock Index" is one of the broadest, managing about 1,650 different stocks in varying proportions. The Value Line tracks the overall market with far less volatility than the Dow or NASDAQ indexes. The advantage is a steady growth or decline rate, with few surprises. The disadvantage is that price movements will be "shallower" than the smaller indexes. Fortunately, the Value Line pays (or costs) $100 for every point it moves.

Of the indexes listed in the table above, the S&P 500 Index is the most expensive, requiring a margin deposit of $17,813 per contract. On the upside, it pays $250 per point of movement, but I usually discourage traders from using this index until they have at least $40,000 in their commodities accounts.

The "Maintenance" column in the table is the lowest your margin deposit can go before a margin call is executed. For example, if you have bought a Value Line contract, depositing $4,500, and the market drops ten points, you would owe $1,000, so your deposit would be reduced to $3,500. Since this is below the "minimum maintenance" for this contract, you would receive a margin call for an additional $100. If the funds are available in the account, the call amount would be automatically allocated.

If you plan to trade commodities futures, one of the most important risk-management tactics is to trade no more than half of your account balance at any given time. Some traders only risk a quarter or third of their capital. It is up to you to pick your level of comfort.

A final note about commodities ticker symbols. In the table above, the symbol for the "Dow Jones Average $10" contract is "DJ," but actually, it's just a prefix. The exchange adds a letter of the alphabet representing the contract month, followed by the last digit of the contract year. For example, the December 2002 Dow contract is tracked as "DJZ2."

Timing your trades, to buy at the lows and sell at the highs, is the "holy grail" of commodities investing. There are hundreds of timing theories out there. Some make sense while others are downright "wacky." For example, one well-known trader bought and sold silver futures with the *moon* - yes, that rock in Earth's orbit - buying on a full moon and selling on a new moon. I think this one needs no further comment.

Since index funds are tied to the overall stock market, and, thus, are reflections of what the public is doing, this strategy does not attempt to *predict* the general trends, but simply confirms and then *reacts* to the trends. The charts make it relatively easy, although they rarely get me the lowest-low entry and highest-high exit points, which is to be expected of any timing method. Most online commodities brokers provide charts for all the contract products and for each contract month, in just about any tick-frequency you could want. For example, my long-term charts use monthly ticks, whereas my trade-timing charts show weekly or daily ticks. The key is that, once you know the long-term trend, based on the "fiscal cycle" we have exposed, you can watch for very familiar chart patterns with reasonable certainty of their outcome.

So, based upon long-term statistics, we know that we want to buy an index fund contract somewhere near the low reached in the September-to-October period. Then, we want to ride the uptrend through the New Year and as far into the spring or summer as the trend takes us, selling our contract the moment it "breaks through" the upward trend line. However, if we miss the bottom or the top - as we will quite often - it is important to have a "fail-safe" date by which to either force the trade or not trade at all.

I have found that a reliable fail-safe purchase date is at the close of trading during any of the last three trading days of October. Since brokers let you order your trade to be filled "at the close," this is not an unusual request. However, it's better to buy - if possible - at the breakout from the previous downtrend. I use both daily and weekly charts to plot these timing trends, drawing a straight line touching the *tops* of the weekly ticks on a downtrend; or drawing a line touching the *bottoms* of the weekly ticks on an uptrend. When the price breaks *across* my trend line, then it's time to take action. Once you have at least three weekly ticks in the trend, you can begin to "project" where the line will be broken.

Figure 6-10 is a weekly chart showing the important downtrends leading to a breakout in September or October. Note specifically the trend line I drew in the fall of 2002 from a high at the week ending September 6th and downward. The breakout occurred near the end of October when the Dow rose to 8000 points.

While a "fail-safe" date (in late-October) for buying the index is statistically reliable, using a "fail-safe" date for exiting is difficult. We have already established that the top will be reached in the month of July about 40 percent of the time, thus, it is logical to use July as a final "fail-safe" exit month, *assuming your uptrend line has not been broken in a prior month*. However, cycle highs are reached in March-20 percent of the time, April-11 percent, May-13 percent, and June-12 percent.

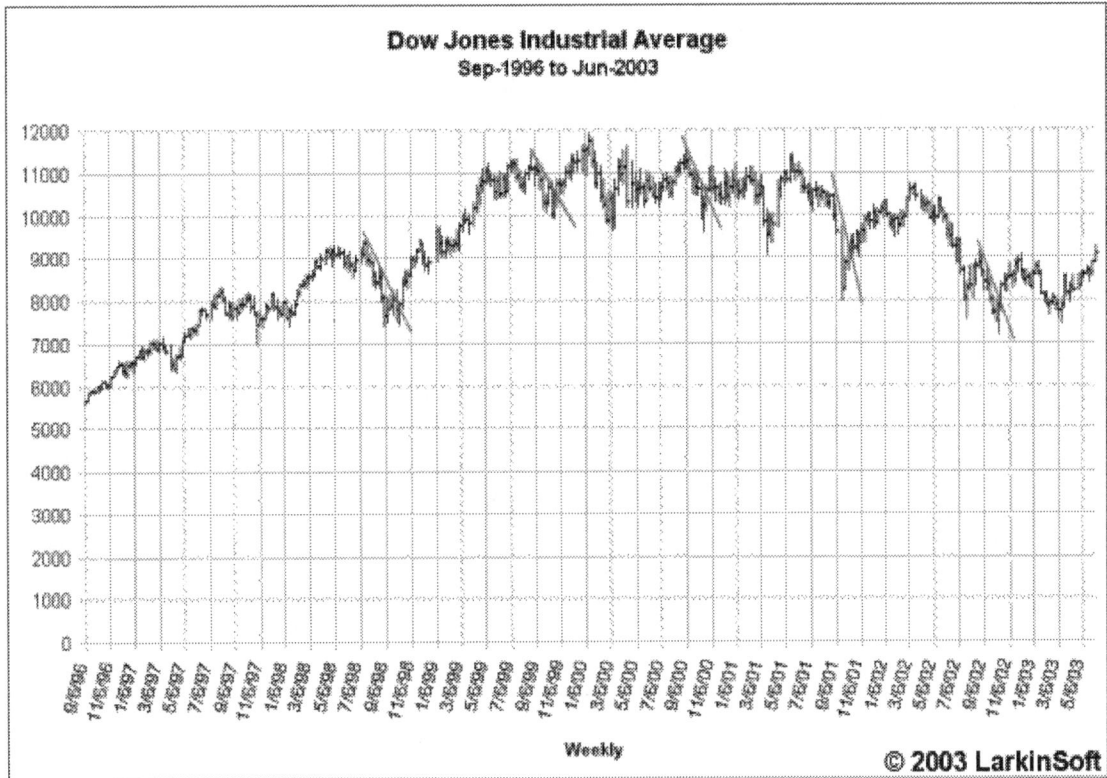

FIGURE 6-10. Dow Jones^{SM} Industrial Average, weekly chart with major downtrends. [Reproduced with permission of Larkin Industries, Inc. © 2003 by LarkinSoft. LarkinSoft is a trademark of Larkin Industries, Inc.]

Exiting your trade requires a cold, objective attitude. If you are well in the black by May, you will either be feeling euphoric and greedy, or euphoric and scared of losing it back. Of course, either way, you are euphoric. If the market is flat in May, you will feel uncertain. If your index dips into the red, you will either feel anxious about losing more or will be even more determined to "hold on" for that last big summer rally. Regardless of which feeling you experience, your trade will be "in the red."

The exit strategy you choose can be based upon trend mathematics, percentage profit, chart trend-line breakouts, trailing stops, or other devices. What's important is: **you must have an exit strategy!** Without one, you risk your entire investment, and potentially more.

At this point, I must distinguish between the actual Dow Jones^{SM} Industrial Average (DJIA) charts and quotes used so far in this chapter, and the charts or quotes you will encounter if you trade the Dow Jones Index Futures contracts through the Chicago Board of Trade (CBOT). The DJIA is a "continuous" index, measured to the nearest penny. The Dow Index futures contracts traded at the CBOT have expiration dates in March, June, September and December, and are each traded as separate products. This means that a November 10, 2002 closing price in the December Dow may be different than the same day's closing price in the following March's contract. In addition, the "Dow" prices for a December contract may actually be higher or lower than the *real* Dow (DJIA) in December. Finally, futures contracts trade in whole points - there are no fractions. Starting with the chart in Figure 6-11, the remainder of this chapter will use the actual futures contract data, except where noted.

Making the Futures Trade

I always use chart trend-lines to help guide my trading activities. The precision of my charting, however, diminishes when the market is very volatile, such as during generally bearish markets. The Dow charts in this chapter illustrate my point. During an overall downtrend, the weekly and monthly highs and lows are widely spaced, while bullish trends seem to be relatively "calm" with narrower ticks. Why is this important? *The taller the tick, the farther your trend line will be from the "ideal" buy or sell price.* In these circumstances, especially, I supplement my charting with other intelligence.

Trend mathematics often helps to validate the breakouts I see on my charts while helping me get the lowest price possible. During a volatile market, the more evidence I can mount, the safer I feel about my trade. While some traders might use a 10- or 20-day average of the highs, looking for an even higher-high as the breakout signal, *I use a 10-day average of daily lows.* Of course, I don't even begin tracking this average until mid-September or early October, and the definitive downtrend can be readily seen on my chart. For example, the 2002-2003 Dow cycle was typical of a volatile market, as illustrated in the *daily* chart below (Figure 6-11). I have drawn two downtrend lines showing the trading range leading to the beginning of the next stock market cycle.

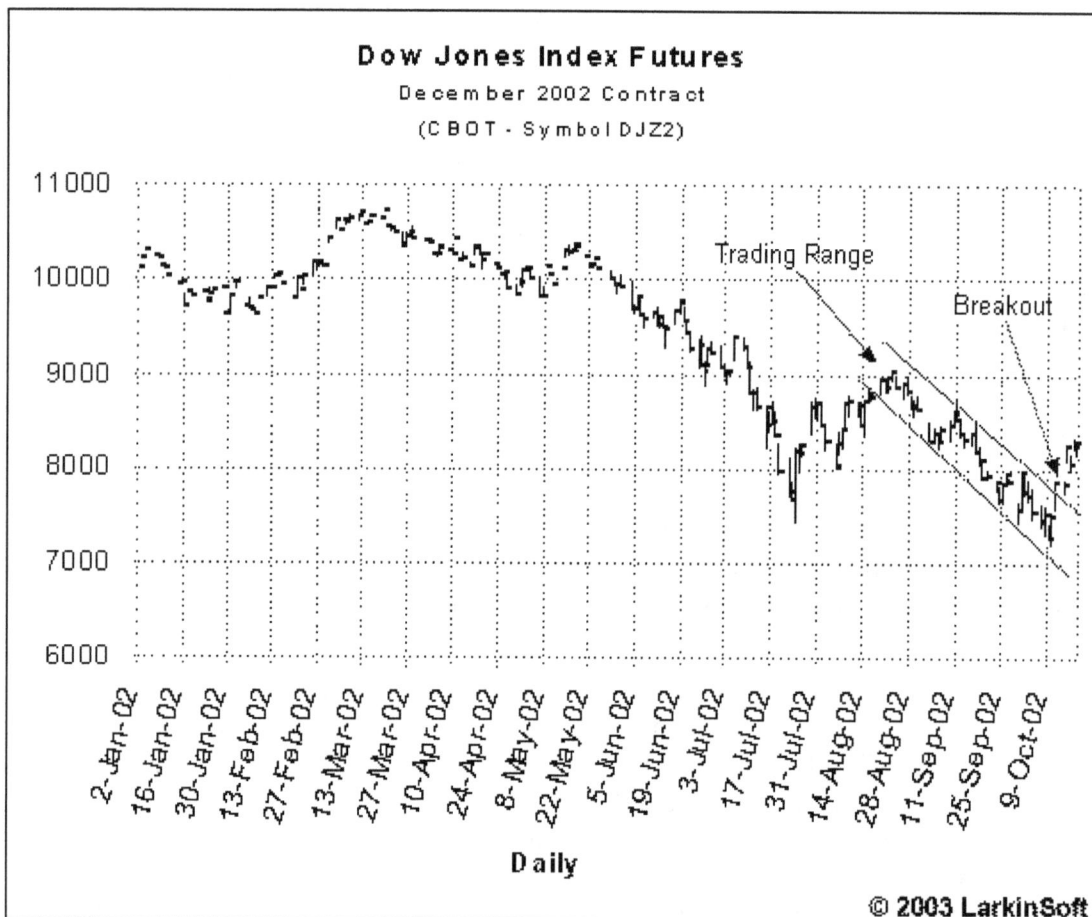

FIGURE 6-11. December 2002 (CBOT) Dow Jones Index Futures, Daily chart, with trend lines added to show breakout of new cycle. [Reproduced with permission of Larkin Industries, Inc. © 2003 by LarkinSoft. LarkinSoft is a trademark of Larkin Industries, Inc.]

Now, see the weekly chart for the same contract (Figure 6-12), and notice the "smoothing" effect a lower-frequency chart has on the data.

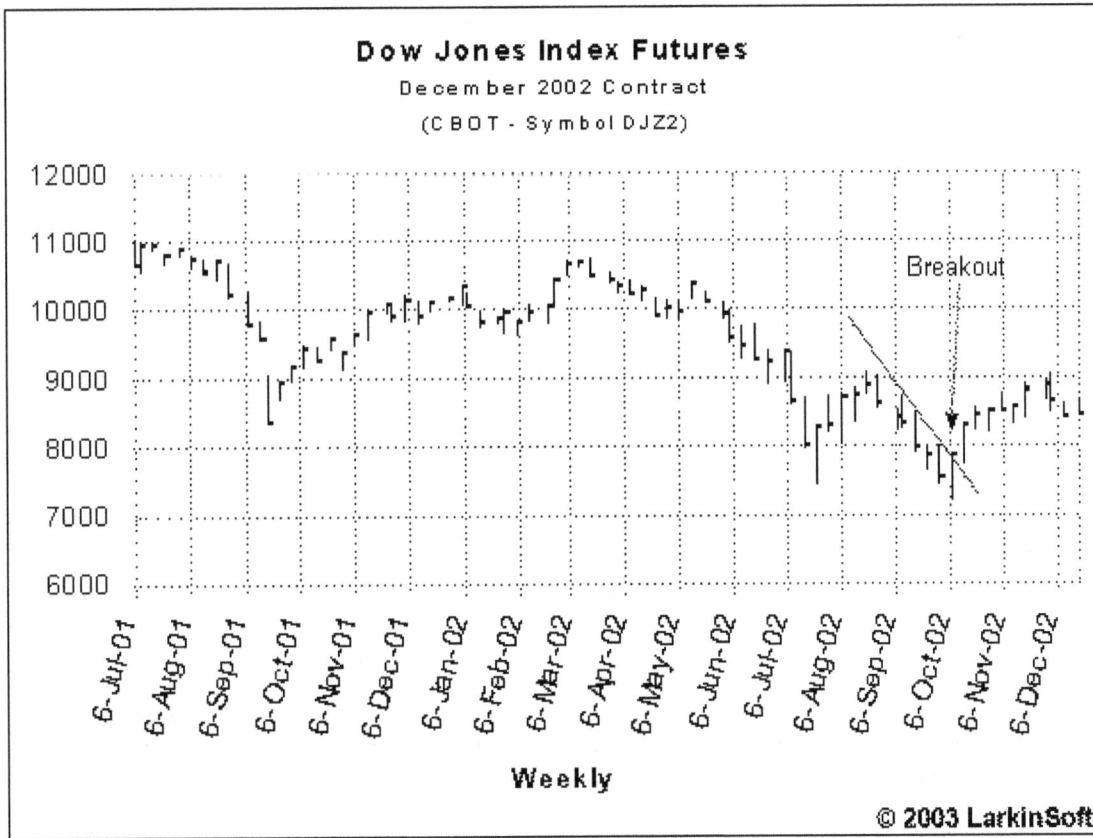

FIGURE 6-12. December 2002 (CBOT) Dow Jones Index Futures, Weekly chart, with trend line added to show breakout of new cycle. [Reproduced with permission of Larkin Industries, Inc. © 2003 by LarkinSoft. LarkinSoft is a trademark of Larkin Industries, Inc.]

On both the daily and weekly chart, you can see that the "breakout" above the "tops" is a reliable signal of a trend reversal. Based upon our "stock market fiscal cycle" philosophy, we would assume that this breakout means the beginning of a new cycle. In fact, I **did** make that assumption, and here's how I traded it.

On Tuesday, October 1, 2002, I began tracking and averaging the previous ten daily lows in a simple worksheet table[94] (see Figure 6-13). *Note that this was ten trading days, not ten calendar days.* My goal was to buy at the close of trading on the day following the "breakout" from my table. Why at the close of trading? Statistics indicate that, during a steep downtrend, closing prices tend to be nearer the daily lows, while in a steep uptrend, closing prices tend to be nearer the daily highs.

---

[94] I used Microsoft Excel, but any spreadsheet software will do.

Dow Jones Index Futures December 2002 Contract (DJZ2) 10-Day Average of Daily Lows			
Date	Daily Low	10-Day Avg	Break?
17-Sep-02	8170	--	--
18-Sep-02	8035	--	--
19-Sep-02	7905	--	--
20-Sep-02	7895	--	--
23-Sep-02	7765	--	--
24-Sep-02	7640	--	--
25-Sep-02	7640	--	--
26-Sep-02	7841	--	--
27-Sep-02	7850	--	--
30-Sep-02	7430	--	--
1-Oct-02	7565	7817	--
2-Oct-02	7710	7756	--
3-Oct-02	7660	7724	--
4-Oct-02	7450	7699	--
7-Oct-02	7385	7655	--
8-Oct-02	7310	7617	--
9-Oct-02	7255	7584	--
10-Oct-02	7180	7545	--
11-Oct-02	7566	7479	BREAK

FIGURE 6-13. Ten-day average of daily lows in the December 2002 Dow (DJZ2). The "BREAK" occurred when the daily low on 11-Oct-2002 exceeded the ten-day average.

On Friday, October 11th, the low for the day was 7566, which was higher than the average of the previous ten lows (7479). As it turns out, the actual low for the entire September-October period had already happened the previous day, at 7180. On Monday, the 14th, the contract opened at 7775, posting a high of 7895 and a low of 7730, then closing at 7858. The brokers usually start trading the "at close" orders within the final five minutes of the trading day, and my buy order was filled at 7859. The margin deposit for a December 2002 Dow Jones $10 Futures contract was $5,400, and my commission was $35 for a round-trip.[95]

You may be wondering: if you expect a rally to extend well into 2003, why would you buy the December 2002 contract month? The reason is "liquidity." Since the Dow index has only been trading at the CBOT since 1997, there are not a lot of speculators trading the far-off contract months until they are within three or four months of expiration. If you buy a "near month" contract, and you wish to continue trading beyond its expiration, you are allowed to "rollover" the contract to the next available month. Your broker would simply re-allocate your margin deposit to the new contract and charge you another round-trip commission. In my case, a possible extra $35 commission was worth the price of guaranteeing that my order got filled. Lately, a near-month Dow contract trades between 10,000 and 30,000 contracts per day. Far months are lucky to move a dozen contracts per day.

---

[95] The term "round-trip" is broker talk for a commission that covers both the buy and the sell. In commodities, the trader pre-pays both ends of the transaction.

Another way to approach the liquidity issue is to use the near-month contract for purposes of charting and timing the trade, but to use a later month as the actual contract you buy. For this example, I could have used my December 2002 Dow chart for timing, but then actually traded the June or September 2003 contract. This would have saved me some potential commissions, but would not have guaranteed me sufficient liquidity in the event I had to sell early.

Now, came the tough part: *waiting*. Unfortunately, my trade never made it to the New Year. The chart in Figure 6-14 tells the story. Since December and early-January are usually positive months for the Dow, I rarely worry about my uptrend line being broken until mid-January. Now, just because I don't *worry* about it doesn't mean I don't *track* it! I began to plot my trend line on the weekly chart in mid-November, and could actually see a nice straight rise along many of the weekly bottoms. Projecting that line into the future, I saw the potential breakout points for the coming weeks. Of course, plotting those points on a chart is one thing, setting stops or other exit maneuvers is another.

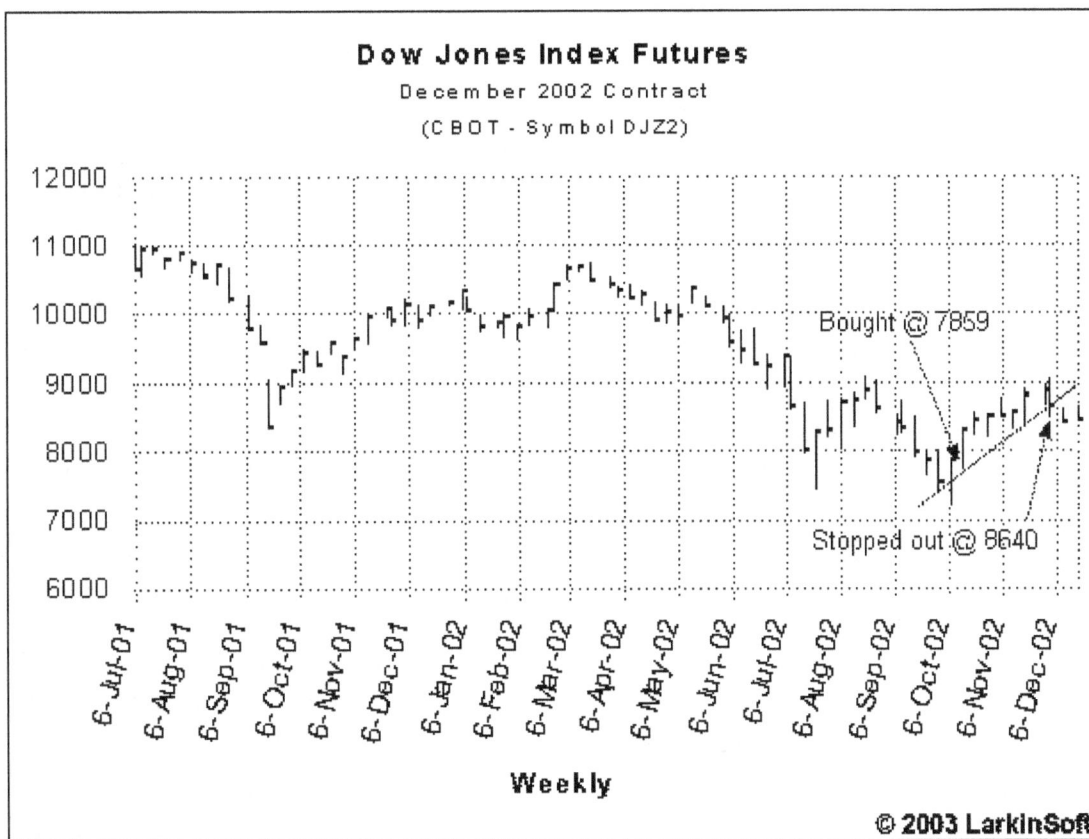

FIGURE 6-14. December 2002 (CBOT) Dow Jones Index Futures, Weekly chart, marked to show the completed trade. [Reproduced with permission of Larkin Industries, Inc. © 2003 by LarkinSoft. LarkinSoft is a trademark of Larkin Industries, Inc.]

On Friday, November 22nd, my Dow contract closed at 8796, up 937 points from my purchase. This was a faster rise than expected (although I wasn't complaining). Sometimes, a quick rise means that speculators will be taking profits prematurely, temporarily stalling the rally. Just in case, I decided to protect my profits above the 100-percent level (544 points, including commissions), so I placed a "trailing stop" on my Dow contract at 400 points below market, thinking I would narrow the gap each week until I got stopped out. I activated the "trail" on Monday the 25th (see Figure 6-15).

Dow Jones Index Futures December 2002 Contract (DJZ2) 400-Point Trailing Stop			
Date	High	Trailing Stop	Low
25-Nov-02	8870	8470	8751
26-Nov-02	8835	8470	8660
27-Nov-02	8940	8540	8710
29-Nov-02	8962	8562	8861
2-Dec-02	9040	8640	8780
3-Dec-02	8855	8640	8720
4-Dec-02	8814	8640	8645
5-Dec-02	8818	8640	8605

FIGURE 6-15. The mechanics of a Trailing Stop.

Some brokers will do trailing stops and some will not. Some brokers let you set trailing stops from their websites and others require that you call it in. As long as the Dow continued to rise, my trailing stop would stay 400 points behind the highest highs. If, however, the market reversed, the stop would remain at its highest level. Then, if the market price came down through my stop, a sell order would automatically be executed at the next available market price.

By the time I got stopped out, my "trail" had risen to 8640 points. It is a rare event to actually be filled at the stop price. Usually, it goes through the price and is filled a point to two beyond. For some reason, my trailing stop was executed, a market order was automatically placed to sell my contract, and at the moment it was to be filled, the Dow had risen back to exactly 8640. No complaints from *me*!

This trade earned 781 points, at $10 apiece, grossing $7,810 and netting $7,775 after commission; or 144 percent profits in just 52 days. Upon liquidation of the contract, my brokerage released the $5,400 margin deposit back to the account. Since the contract was sold before its expiration (scheduled for December 18th), I didn't have to pay a "rollover" commission. In fact, the only "downside" to this trade was that I would now owe capital gains taxes within the same year on these profits. Again, I wasn't complaining!

Although I got stopped out early, I was still expecting the Dow to rally through the summer of 2003, so I was pretty sure that there would be another entry opportunity. But, I would have to wait for a new downtrend to materialize, then hit bottom, and then breakout.

The trade I have described may seem complicated to some, requiring some charting, averaging, setting stops, and so on. But, fortunately, there is only one "stock market cycle" each year, so the work is minimal. The potential rewards make the relative "complexity" worthwhile.

One of the choices I could have made in October 2002 was to stay in my original contract, rolling it over to March 2003, covering any margin calls, rolling it again to the June contract and hoping for a big summer rally. That decision would have been based upon two factors: the amount of funds in my account, and my tolerance for risk. As of this writing, the Dow is near 9,200 points, nearly 560 points above my December stop, and still rising. The current uptrend "broke out" in late March 2003. To complete the "cycle," I expect that the market will top out in the late-June to early-August period, and drop sharply to a low in September or October. Sound familiar?

So far, I have described one method of trading index funds on the commodities market. But, there is another "option" you can take - literally!

Simplify and Protect Your Trades

Now that I've described how futures trading works and given an example of how to capitalize on the stock market "cycle," let me offer a simpler method of doing the same thing, without the threat of a margin call: by trading "options on futures."

If you're not familiar with options, let me briefly explain. An option is simply an instrument that gives you the right to buy or sell a futures contract by a certain date at a certain price. You are under no obligation to actually buy or sell the futures contract - that "option" is yours. When you buy an option for the right to "buy long" a futures contract, it is a "call" option. When you buy an option for the right to "sell short" a futures contract, it is a "put" option. In either case, you "buy" the option.

The cost of an option is a one-time, non-refundable "premium," and will vary depending upon the amount of time left before the option's expiration date, and the value of the underlying futures contract. *The advantage of an option is that the premium you pay is the limit of your capital risk.* If the market goes against you, the premium value of your option may shrink to Zero, but it will never go into the red. On the other hand, your potential for profit is exactly the same as if you had bought or sold the futures contract represented by the option.

An option stipulates the price at which you will buy or sell the underlying futures contract. This is called a "strike" price. For example, if you believe the Dow will have peaked in 2003 at, say, 9400 points, you could either "sell short" a futures contract, or you could buy a "put" option with a 9000-point strike price (or thereabouts). The premium for a "December 2003 Dow 9000 Put Option," as of this writing, was around $4,500, which is cheaper than the deposit for a Dow futures contract (but non-refundable).

If the market continues upward, the premium value of your "put" option will go down. However, if the Dow does begin its downward slide toward a September-October low, and passes the 9000-point mark, your option would now be considered "in the money" and you would have the opportunity to "exercise" it, which means converting it to the actual futures contract.

The reason they call it an "option," though, is that you are not *required* to exercise it. Besides, once your option is "in the money," its premium value will rise or fall by the exact same amount that the underlying futures contract does. If the futures contract gains $1,000, so will your option value. Thus, in many cases, you may not want to exercise the option even though it is "in the money." Instead, you might want to just sell the option and pocket the profits above your original premium. If you do decide to exercise the option, your protection against future margin calls will no longer exist - a further reason to just hold on to the option.

Whether your option is "in the money" or not, you can "liquidate" your option at any time prior to its expiration date. If, at the time of liquidation, the option is "in the money," you will make at least the value of the underlying futures contract, plus any remaining "premium" value. If, at the time of liquidation, the option has not yet reached its strike price, you will only receive its current "premium" value.

For example, let's return to my Dow trade back in October 2002. When the Dow broke out of its low at around 7900 points, instead of buying a futures contract, I could have estimated that the Dow would reach 8500 or 9000 by the following summer, and could have bought a "September 2003 Dow Jones Index 9000 Call Option." My premium would have been in the neighborhood of $5,000, representing the sum-total of my risk (plus commission). I would not have to worry about stop-losses, or trailing stops, or uptrend lines, or ten-day averages. My only concern would have been *time*. If the strike price had not been met by the option's expiration date, the option would expire worthless. This is the only major risk of using options. Statistically, about 80 percent of all options expire worthless, but there are two ways of minimizing that risk:

1. **Buy options with expiration dates beyond your expected liquidation date; and**

2. **Buy options with strike prices at ("in the money") or near the·current market price.**

In the case of our stock market cycle, we believe that the bottom will occur by the end of October and the top will occur no later than July or August. So, buying the September contract month for the following year will usually give the process enough time to "capture" the cycle highs. Next, if the Dow has been averaging at least 1,000 points of gain in past cycles, you would want to buy your Call option at a strike price *within* 1,000 points of the current market. Your broker (or his website) can tell you what strike prices are available and the premium cost at each strike. Some traders prefer to pay a little extra and buy options that are already "in the money." The advantage is that they start earning profits immediately at the same rate as the underlying futures contract.

If we are nearing the end of the stock market cycle, and the market has topped out, and has since been dropping steadily toward a September-October low, you could then buy a "put" option on a December Dow contract with a strike price at, or below, the current market. Again, with no risk of a margin call, your upside profit potential would be as good as if you had "sold short" a futures contract. This additional strategy would allow you to "double dip," earning profits in *both* "cycle" directions. After all: what goes up, must come down (unless it orbits).

Shorting the Stock Market Cycle

During the period 1930 through 2002, statistics show that the Dow Jones[SM] Industrial Average dropped from its high in the spring or summer to a low in September or October in all but three years. The statistics also show that, during the current bear market (2000-2002), the recorded drop during the end-of-cycle period is substantial. The tables below (starting with Figure 6-16) measure the "drop" for each cycle since 1930. Note that the three failing years were still within two percent of "breaking even."

As you can see in Figure 6-18, during bear markets (such as the 2000-2002 era), the number of points lost by the Dow through the "end-of-cycle" date exceeded the previously recorded "cycle gains" (see Figure 6-8). If you had been "shorting" the Dow during these periods, your overall returns would have been substantially higher than simply trading the Dow in one direction.

The problem with predicting the stock market, of course, is one can never really know where and when the true top or true bottom will occur. However, based upon our statistical analysis dating back to 1930, we can see **a recurring pattern with 95.83 percent reliability** (three failures in 72 years). *This reliability climbs to 100 percent within the past 20 years of statistics* (Figure 6-18).

Dow Jones Industrial Average End-of-Cycle Statistics - 1930 to 1955						
Period	Cycle High	High Value	End of Cycle	End Value	Net Drop	% Drop
1930-1931	2-Mar-31	191.90	5-Oct-31	85.50	(106.40)	55.45%
1931-1932	8-Mar-32	89.90	10-Oct-32	57.70	(32.20)	35.82%
1932-1933	18-Jul-33	110.50	20-Oct-33	83.60	(26.90)	24.34%
1933-1934	20-Apr-34	107.00	17-Sep-34	85.70	(21.30)	19.91%
1934-1935	31-Jul-35	127.00	3-Oct-35	127.00	0.00	0.00%
1935-1936	28-Jul-36	168.20	17-Sep-36	164.80	(3.40)	2.02%
1936-1937	10-Mar-37	195.60	19-Oct-37	115.80	(79.80)	40.80%
1937-1938	25-Jul-38	146.30	26-Sep-38	127.90	(18.40)	12.58%
1938-1939	10-Mar-39	152.70	18-Sep-39	147.40	(5.30)	3.47%
1939-1940	8-Apr-40	152.10	13-Sep-40	127.20	(24.90)	16.37%
1940-1941	22-Jul-41	131.10	31-Oct-41	117.40	(13.70)	10.45%
1941-1942	15-Jul-42	109.50	11-Sep-42	105.60	(3.90)	3.56%
1942-1943	15-Jul-43	146.40	13-Oct-43	135.90	(10.50)	7.17%
1943-1944	10-Jul-44	150.90	14-Sep-44	142.70	(8.20)	5.43%
1944-1945	26-Jun-45	169.60	17-Sep-45	173.30	3.70	-2.18%
1945-1946	29-May-46	213.40	30-Oct-46	160.50	(52.90)	24.79%
1946-1947	25-Jul-47	187.70	26-Sep-47	174.40	(13.30)	7.09%
1947-1948	14-Jun-48	194.50	27-Sep-48	175.80	(18.70)	9.61%
1948-1949	30-Mar-49	179.20	20-Sep-49	177.60	(1.60)	0.89%
1949-1950	12-Jun-50	229.20	6-Sep-50	217.40	(11.80)	5.15%
1950-1951	4-May-51	264.40	29-Oct-51	256.40	(8.00)	3.03%
1951-1952	31-Jul-52	280.30	23-Oct-52	262.00	(18.30)	6.53%
1952-1953	18-Mar-53	292.00	15-Sep-53	254.40	(37.60)	12.88%
1953-1954	30-Jul-54	349.20	10-Sep-54	345.50	(3.70)	1.06%
1954-1955	26-Jul-55	471.70	11-Oct-55	433.20	(38.50)	8.16%
1955-1956	9-Apr-56	524.40	1-Oct-56	463.80	(60.60)	11.56%

FIGURE 6-16. Dow Jones[SM] Industrial Average (DJIA) End-of-Cycle Statistics, 1930-1955. [Reproduced with permission of Larkin Industries, Inc. © 2003 by LarkinSoft. LarkinSoft is a trademark of Larkin Industries, Inc.]

As I have mentioned, the investing public, in general, "frowns" on the practice of shorting the market. *Stock Market Mercenaries,* however, must often go against the public sentiment to find profit opportunities.

The process of trading futures and options to capitalize on the market's end-of-cycle drop, is the exact opposite of the process I described in earlier sections. Instead of "buying long" a Dow contract (or other market index fund), we "sell short" a futures contract, thereby profiting on the "losses" suffered by the index. Or, instead of buying "Call" options to reduce risks during the cycle uptrend, we buy "Put" options to reduce risks during the end-of-cycle drop.

Whether you are shorting futures or "putting" options, your goal is to be fully liquidated sometime in September or October of the year. Thus, you should be able to safely use the "December" contract month for either trading futures or options during this period. For example, after seeing the Dow top out on March 8, 2002, at 10729, you could have purchased a "December 2002 Dow Index Put Option" with a 10,000 strike price for between $5,000 and

$6,000. As the market began to drop, your option would have been "in the money" by the end of April, and you would have earned about 3,000 points, or $30,000, when you sold your "put" option in mid-October. By using a "put" option instead of directly selling short a futures contract, you would not have had to worry about margin calls in the event the Dow rallied over the summer. If the Dow *had* risen instead, your option's "premium" value would have diminished temporarily until the real drop occurred. In any case, your premium investment would have been your maximum financial risk.

Dow Jones Industrial Average End-of-Cycle Statistics - 1956 to 1980						
Period	**Cycle High**	**High Value**	**End of Cycle**	**End Value**	**Net Drop**	**% Drop**
1956-1957	16-Jul-57	523.10	22-Oct-57	416.20	(106.90)	20.44%
1957-1958	31-Jul-58	508.40	10-Sep-58	514.60	6.20	-1.22%
1958-1959	30-Jul-59	678.70	22-Sep-59	613.30	(65.40)	9.64%
1959-1960	9-Jun-60	663.60	25-Oct-60	564.20	(99.40)	14.98%
1960-1961	22-May-61	714.70	25-Sep-61	688.90	(25.80)	3.61%
1961-1962	16-Mar-62	727.10	24-Oct-62	549.70	(177.40)	24.40%
1962-1963	5-Jun-63	733.00	30-Sep-63	728.60	(4.40)	0.60%
1963-1964	20-Jul-64	855.20	10-Sep-64	852.70	(2.50)	0.29%
1964-1965	14-May-65	944.80	10-Sep-65	911.70	(33.10)	3.50%
1965-1966	21-Apr-66	961.90	10-Oct-66	735.70	(226.20)	23.52%
1966-1967	21-Jul-67	918.70	31-Oct-67	876.20	(42.50)	4.63%
1967-1968	3-May-68	935.70	12-Sep-68	908.10	(27.60)	2.95%
1968-1969	14-May-69	974.90	9-Oct-69	794.00	(180.90)	18.56%
1969-1970	25-Mar-70	803.30	22-Sep-70	741.50	(61.80)	7.69%
1970-1971	28-Apr-71	958.10	28-Oct-71	827.80	(130.30)	13.60%
1971-1972	30-May-72	979.50	17-Oct-72	917.10	(62.40)	6.37%
1972-1973	8-Mar-73	985.30	14-Sep-73	873.30	(112.00)	11.37%
1973-1974	14-Mar-74	904.00	4-Oct-74	573.20	(330.80)	36.59%
1974-1975	15-Jul-75	888.90	1-Oct-75	780.50	(108.40)	12.19%
1975-1976	24-Mar-76	1018.00	12-Oct-76	928.30	(89.70)	8.81%
1976-1977	16-Mar-77	971.60	25-Oct-77	792.80	(178.80)	18.40%
1977-1978	6-Jun-78	879.30	30-Oct-78	782.10	(97.20)	11.05%
1978-1979	11-Apr-79	884.60	22-Oct-79	796.00	(88.60)	10.02%
1979-1980	30-Jul-80	946.90	31-Oct-80	911.60	(35.30)	3.73%
1980-1981	27-Apr-81	1031.00	28-Sep-81	807.50	(223.50)	21.68%

FIGURE 6-17. Dow Jones[SM] Industrial Average (DJIA) End-of-Cycle Statistics, 1956-1980. [Reproduced with permission of Larkin Industries, Inc. © 2003 by LarkinSoft. LarkinSoft is a trademark of Larkin Industries, Inc.]

In the 72-year period from 1931 through 2002, the number of points lost by the Dow during this end-of-cycle drop, was *at least* 10 percent of the earlier cycle gains 89 percent of the time. The drop was at least 25 percent of the earlier gain 72 percent of the time; and at least 50 percent of the earlier gain 51 percent of the time. Why are these statistics useful? Because, if you plan to use options, your goal should be to pick option strike prices with a reasonable chance of being "struck!"

Dow Jones Industrial Average End-of-Cycle Statistics - 1981 to 2002						
Period	Cycle High	High Value	End of Cycle	End Value	Net Drop	% Drop
1981-1982	7-May-82	876.50	30-Sep-82	891.30	14.80	-1.69%
1982-1983	17-Jun-83	1260.70	16-Sep-83	1210.20	(50.50)	4.01%
1983-1984	16-Mar-84	1197.20	10-Oct-84	1158.20	(39.00)	3.26%
1984-1985	23-Jul-85	1372.20	18-Sep-85	1283.70	(88.50)	6.45%
1985-1986	2-Jul-86	1922.70	29-Sep-86	1733.00	(189.70)	9.87%
1986-1987	31-Jul-87	2588.30	20-Oct-87	1616.20	(972.10)	37.56%
1987-1988	6-Jul-88	2169.50	13-Sep-88	2055.30	(114.20)	5.26%
1988-1989	31-Jul-89	2668.30	16-Oct-89	2496.90	(171.40)	6.42%
1989-1990	17-Jul-90	3024.30	11-Oct-90	2344.30	(680.00)	22.48%
1990-1991	3-Jun-91	3057.50	9-Oct-91	2925.50	(132.00)	4.32%
1991-1992	2-Jun-92	3435.30	5-Oct-92	3087.40	(347.90)	10.13%
1992-1993	27-Jul-93	3604.90	21-Sep-93	3501.50	(103.40)	2.87%
1993-1994	18-Mar-94	3911.80	5-Oct-94	3736.20	(175.60)	4.49%
1994-1995	27-Jul-95	4768.00	10-Oct-95	4638.40	(129.60)	2.72%
1995-1996	23-May-96	5833.00	10-Sep-96	5681.70	(151.30)	2.59%
1996-1997	31-Jul-97	8329.00	28-Oct-97	6936.50	(1392.50)	16.72%
1997-1998	17-Jul-98	9412.60	8-Oct-98	7399.80	(2012.80)	21.38%
1998-1999	19-Jul-99	11321.60	18-Oct-99	9884.20	(1437.40)	12.70%
1999-2000	12-Apr-00	11600.40	18-Oct-00	9571.40	(2029.00)	17.49%
2000-2001	21-May-01	11436.40	21-Sep-01	7926.90	(3509.50)	30.69%
2001-2002	8-Mar-02	10728.90	10-Oct-02	7181.47	(3547.43)	33.06%

FIGURE 6-18. Dow Jones[SM] Industrial Average (DJIA) End-of-Cycle Statistics, 1981-2002. [Reproduced with permission of Larkin Industries, Inc. © 2003 by LarkinSoft. LarkinSoft is a trademark of Larkin Industries, Inc.]

For example, in the 1999-2000 cycle, the Dow gained 1,716 points when it topped out at 11,600 on April 12, 2000. A cautious trader might have picked a strike price of 25 percent of the gains, or 429 points, and deducted the points from the Dow's highest level, yielding 11,171. Since most Dow option strike prices are offered in increments divisible by 100, a strike of 11,200, 11,100, or 11,000 might have been available. Buying a "December Dow 2000 Put Option" at an 11,000 strike in April or May would have yielded at least 1,400 points by the low in mid-October, resulting in a $14,000 gross return.

Remember, the closer the strike price is to the current market, the sooner you begin to profit, as if you were holding the underlying futures contract. Had our "cautious" trader bought his option at an 11,500 strike in April 2000, he would have made a higher profit from those extra 500 Dow points (at $10 apiece). Of course, the option premium would have been higher for that privilege!

In our great capitalist system, making a profit is as "American" as apple pie and baseball. As long as that profit can be made legally and honestly, *Stock Market Mercenaries* must be equipped to profit in any way possible from the markets. It doesn't matter that shorting the market carries a negative stigma in the public's eye. Ninety-three percent of the public loses money in the market, so that "stigma" is irrelevant!

Money Management in Commodities

Generally, trading in futures and options carries a higher risk than investing directly in the stock market. By trading in contracts tied to stock market indexes, we can lower risks through the inherent diversification of those indexes. By trading those indexes through the commodities market, we can leverage our capital to achieve incredible annual profits. So, what's the catch?

Recognize Your Risk

Unless you plan to trade exclusively in options, where your total risk can be easily calculated in advance, you will need a significant amount of capital to trade futures with relative safety. In fact, I urge you to consider using options for your first few trades, until your charting and trading skills warrant the extra risk of trading straight futures.

Additionally, if you plan to short the market during its end-of-cycle drop, you may also want to exercise greater caution, especially during long-term bull markets. Employ the same caution during long-term bear markets at the breakouts for the start-of-cycle rally. One way to back-up that caution is through the use of options rather than futures, especially when shorting the market. If you are trading in futures, always use stop losses or trailing stops to protect your gains and minimize your potential margin calls. If you are trading in options, always pick a strike price close to the current market, and pick an expiration month beyond the normal end to the "cycle" you are trading.

Capital Limits

If you are new to commodities trading, you should not even consider investing in futures and options until you have at least $20,000 you can cheerfully lose. It only takes one big margin call, or your options expiring worthless, to wipe out your capital.

Further, you should never risk more than 50 percent (give or take a little) of the available cash in your commodities account. If you follow the *Leveraged Index Fund Strategy*, your potential returns should - with rare exception - allow your account to grow rapidly despite only *half* of your capital being invested at any given time.

When you make a profit, be sure to plan for the resulting capital gains tax you will owe. Some traders automatically withdraw from their commodities account a percentage of their profits every year to cover their taxes. Others pay their taxes from other sources of income, leaving their profits in the account to be reinvested (and compounded). Hopefully, you will soon be faced with this dilemma!

Paper Trading

The same case for paper trading that we made in Chapter 5 applies to commodities trading. I strongly recommend that you paper trade the *Leveraged Index Fund Strategy* before committing a single penny of your wealth to the cause. Fortunately, most online commodities brokers offer simulated trading systems, allowing you to "play around" with your strategies until you're comfortable with the process.

Your paper-trading activities should include charting, calculating averages, setting stop-losses and trailing stops, and every other "device" covered in this chapter. Become familiar with the commodities "culture" by reading books and by visiting brokerage and exchange websites. There are many online sources of education on commodities trading, and much of this information is available for free.

Most of the charts and trading examples used in this chapter were focused on the Dow Jones^{SM} Industrial Average indexes. However, much broader indexes, such as the S&P 500 and the Value Line, can offer an even higher level of diversification, while still allowing for leveraged returns through the commodities exchanges. Paper trading allows you to practice on many indexes simultaneously, thereby accelerating your education.

Summary

Whereas the modified *Investolator*® method in Chapter 5 offers *Stock Market Mercenaries* a powerful "machine gun," the *Leveraged Index Fund Strategy* arms you with the "heavy artillery" you need to profit from the *big picture* in the stock market. You now have the tools to trade individual stocks, or an entire index full of stocks, and profit by doing what the public rarely does: "buy cheap and sell dear."

You have learned how to limit and manage your risk of loss through trading techniques and the proper use of options. Further, you have learned that the U.S. stock market operates in a recurring cycle of highs and lows, which can be harnessed to generate high returns with relatively low risk.

You are now equipped to make money from the stock market no matter which direction it chooses to go.

Conclusion

If your goal is to play in Wall Street, the world's largest casino, you must come to the table with the keys to survival and profit. You must be wary of advice offered from any source; be willing to do your homework; and have iron-masked control of your emotions. You must be willing to buy when the public is selling, and sell when the public is buying. Finally, to consistently profit in this game, you must exceed the returns that most people think are "sufficient," because you must overcome the manipulators, the taxman, and the inflation drain on your wealth, *before* you will gain a cent.

To be a *Stock Market Mercenary*, your actions must be strictly profit-motivated. This may sound "cold" and "uncharitable" to some. So be it! Your opponents are also cold and uncharitable when it comes to relieving you of the "burdens" of accumulating wealth. (Charity comes later, generously supported from the profits you will draw from your account.)

So, you can be one of the 93 percent who lose money every year in the market; and you can be content with the thought of having to work at age 65. Or, you can play the same game the insiders do, and beat them at it. It doesn't take a genius, or "guru," to win this game. It only requires finding the real "winners" in the market and riding their coattails.

Hopefully, this book has given you the insight, the weapons, and the strategies to fight back and win. If so, my mission is complete, and yours has already begun.

Bibliography

Allen, Frederick Lewis. *The Great Pierpont Morgan*. New York: Harper & Brothers, 1949.

Beschloss, Michael R. *Kennedy and Roosevelt: The Uneasy Alliance*. New York: Norton, 1980.

Buffett, Warren. Transcript of speech before New York Society of Security Analysts. December 6, 1994.

Buffett, Warren E. *How Inflation Swindles the Investor*. Fortune, May 5, 1977.

Buffett, Warren. *Investing in Equity Markets*. From seminar transcript, Columbia University Business School, March 13, 1985.

Buffett, Warren. *Berkshire Hathaway Inc - Chairman's Letter - 1996*. February 28, 1997. (www.berkshirehathaway.com/letters/1996.html) Used by permission.

Buffett, Warren. *Berkshire Hathaway Inc - An Owner's Manual*. June, 1996. (www.berkshirehathaway.com/1996ar/manual.html) Used by permission.

Chancellor, Edward. *Devil Take the Hindmost: A History of Financial Speculation*. New York: Farrar, Straus and Giroux, 1999.

Chicago Board of Trade (CBOT). (www.cbot.com)

Chicago Mercantile Exchange (CME). (www.cme.com)

Clavell, James, editor. *The Art of War: Sun Tzu*. edited from translation by Lionel Giles, 1910, Shanghai. New York: Dell Publishing, 1983.

Cleland, Scott. *Global Crossing's Bankruptcy: A Window Into a Broken System of Protecting Investors*. (Testimony before the House Financial Services Oversight Subcommittee) Washington D.C.: Precursor Group®, March 21, 2002. Used with permission of Scott Cleland, founder and CEO of the Precursor Group® and founder and Chairman of the Investorside® Research Association. All rights reserved. (www.precursorgroup.com)

Clews, Henry. *Fifty Years in Wall Street*. New York: Irving Publishing Company, 1908.

Congressional Budget Office. *Perspectives on the Ownership of Capital Assets and the Realization of Capital Gains*. May 1997. (www.cbo.gov)

Dorr, Robert. *Buffett Quickly Unloaded First Three Stock Shares*. Omaha World-Herald, December 5, 1968.

Federal Reserve. *Money Stock and Debt Measures*. March 22, 2001. (www.federalreserve.gov)

Federal Reserve. *H.6 Release - Federal Reserve Board of Governors*. January 15, 2003. (http://research.stlouisfed.org/fred/data/wkly/m3)

Federal Reserve Bank, Cleveland. *Money Growth and Inflation*. PUB Cleveland, July 1999.

Forbes. *The World's Billionaires*. Forbes.com, 2002. (www.forbes.com/2002/02/28/billionaires.html)

Gordon, John Steele. *The Great Game*. New York: Scribner, 1999.

Grant, Linda. *The $4 Billion Regular Guy*. The Los Angeles Times Magazine, April 7, 1991.

Greider, William. *The Secrets of the Temple: How the Federal Reserve Runs the Country*. New York: Simon and Schuster, 1987.

Hughey, Ann. *Omaha's Plain Dealer*. Newsweek, April 1, 1985.

Humes, James C. *Churchill: Speaker of the Century*. New York: Scarborough Books, 1982.

Internal Revenue Service. (www.irs.gov)

IShares. (www.iShares.com)

James, Dan. *Credit: The American Way; Depression: Are We On The Way?* California Grower, November 1987, Vol. XI, No. 11.

Johnson, Jeff. *Union Leaders Accused of Profiting From Insider Trading.* CNSNews.com, Thursday, August 15, 2002. (www.CNSNews.com)

Kansas City Board of Trade (KCBT). (www.kcbt.com)

Koskoff, David E. *Joseph P. Kennedy: A Life and Times.* Englewood Cliffs, NJ: Prentice-Hall, Inc., 1974.

Lane, Wheaton. *Commodore Vanderbilt, an Epic of the Steam Age.* New York: Knopf, 1942.

Lefevre, Edwin. *Reminiscences of a Stock Operator.* New York: Wiley, 1994. (A reprint of the 1923 edition.)

Levitt, Arthur. *SEC Chairman Arthur Levitt, Concerned That the Quality of Corporate Financial Reporting Is Eroding, Announces Action Plan to Remedy Problem.* September 28, 1998. (www.sec.gov/news/press/pressarchive/1998/98-95.txt).

Lowe, Janet. *Benjamin Graham on Value Investing: Lessons from the Dean of Wall Street.* Dearborn, MI: Dearborn Financial Publishing, 1994.

Lowe, Janet. *Warren Buffett Speaks: Wit and Wisdom from the World's Greatest Investor.* New York: John Wiley & Sons, Inc., 1997.

Morgenson, Gretchen. *How Did So Many Get It So Wrong?* New York Times, December 31, 2000.

Morsa, Matt. *A Classic Case of Manipulation.* Grants Pass, OR: The Investolator, October 2000. (1-800-711-8734)

NASDAQ Historical Archives. (www.nasdaq.com)

New York Herald, March 25, 1863.

NewsMax.com. *Gov. Gray Davis' Corporate Sleaze.* NewsMax.com, Wednesday, July 24, 2002.

Paul, Randolph E. *Taxation in the United States.* Boston: Little, Brown, 1954.

PricewaterhouseCoopers Management Barometer. Large Institutional Investors, Though Major Shareholders, Have Limited Influence on Corporate Strategy, PricewaterhouseCoopers Finds. April 4, 2002. (www.barometersurveys.com)

Rasmussen, Jim. *Hometown Deal Pleases Buffett.* Omaha World-Herald, October 21, 1992.

Securities and Exchange Commission. (www.sec.gov)

SEC/Edgar Online. (www.sec.gov/info/edgar.shtml)

Seligman, Joel. *The Transformation of Wall Street: A History of the Securities and Exchange Commission and Modern Corporate Finance.* Boston: Houghton Mifflin, 1982.

Shihoko Goto. *Global Crossing Similar to Enron.* United Press International, Friday, March 22, 2002.

Siconolfi, Michael. *Under Pressure: at Morgan Stanley, Analysts Were Urged to Soften Harsh Views.* Wall Street Journal, July 14, 1992.

Sincere, Michael. *101 Investment Lessons From the Wizards of Wall Street.* Franklin Lakes, NJ: The Career Press, Inc., 1999. Used with permission of the publisher. © 1999 Michael Sincere. All rights reserved.

Sobel, Robert. *The Big Board: A History of the New York Stock Market.* New York: The Free Press, 1965.

Social Security Administration. *Income of the Population 55 or Older, 2000.* (www.ssa.gov)

Sparkes, Boyden and Moore, Samuel Taylor. *The Witch of Wall Street, Hetty Green.* Garden City, NY: Doubleday, Doran and Co., 1935.

The Motley Fool. (www.fool.com)

The Motley Fool. *Dow Investing Explained,* 1998. (www.fool.com/school/dowinvesting.htm)

The New Lexicon Webster's Dictionary of the English Language. New York: Lexicon Publications, Inc., 1988 Edition.

Train, George Francis. *Young America in Wall-Street.* New York: Derby & Jackson, 1857.

U.S. Government Accounting Office. *Securities Markets: Actions Needed to Better Protect Investors against Unscrupulous Brokers.* GAO/GGD-94-208. (www.gao.gov)

Vernon, Wes. *Congress Finally Ready to Investigate Global Crossing.* NewsMax.com, Friday, March 15, 2002. (www.NewsMax.com)

Vernon, Wes. *Lawmakers Attack Global Crossing but Hush Up Political Angle.* NewsMax.com, Friday, March 22, 2002. (www.NewsMax.com)

Vise, David A. and Coll, Steve. *Buffett-watchers Follow Lead of Omaha's Long-term Stock Investor.* The Washington Post, October 2, 1987.

Warren, Ted. *How To Make the Stock Market Make Money For You.* Grants Pass, OR: The Ted Warren Corporation, 1966; 3rd edition, 1998.

Washington Post. *Enron Raised Funds In Private Offering.* January 22, 2002. (www.washingtonpost.com/wp-dyn/articles/A15912-2002Jan21.html)

Weiss, Martin D., PhD. *The Ultimate Safe Money Guide.* New York: John Wiley & Sons, Inc., 2002. Copyright © 2002 Martin D. Weiss, Ph.D. This material is used by permission of John Wiley & Sons, Inc.

Yahoo! Finance. (finance.yahoo.com) Charts and Web screens reproduced with permission of Yahoo! Inc. © 2003 by Yahoo! Inc. YAHOO! and the YAHOO! logo are trademarks of Yahoo! Inc.

Ziegler, Philip. *The Sixth Great Power: A History of One of the Greatest Banking Families, the House of Barings, 1762-1929.* New York: Knopf, 1988.

How to Get More Information From the Author

The author is not in the business of recommending individual stocks or managing other people's portfolios. To do that, he would be required to register his services with the SEC, whose dogma would prevent him from freely recommending the chartist methods described in this book (see Chapter 4). What he *is* in business to do is consult, provide information technology services, trade the markets, and write. Thus, the following services may be of interest to you.

Online Chart Updates

Most of the charts, tables and graphs presented in this book are also published in full color at www.StockMarketMercenary.com. The charts and tables will be updated periodically with current statistics, and may include some of the author's trades not included in this book. This service is for non-commercial, educational purposes only, and may not be used as a stock recommendation service.

Consulting & Hands-on Training

Should you desire detailed, hands-on demonstrations of the methods described in this book, the author can be scheduled for consulting, and personal or group training engagements. If you have questions or feedback about the information in this book, you may e-mail the author at mercenary@dljames.com. Due to the high volume of e-mail received, timely replies are unlikely, but, rest assured your e-mail will be read!

ISBN 0-9742416-8-7

www.ingramcontent.com/pod-product-compliance
Lightning Source LLC
Chambersburg PA
CBHW081508200326
41518CB00015B/2420